Rebels Against Slavery

American Slave Revolts

Patricia C. McKissack
and Fredrick L. McKissack

SCHOLASTIC INC. NEW YORK · TORONTO · LONDON · AUCKLAND · SYDNEY
MEXICO CITY · NEW DELHI · HONG KONG

**DEDICATED TO:
OUR SONS AND
DAUGHTER-IN-LAW,
REBELS ALL**

ISBN 0-590-66259-7

12 11 10 9 8 7 6 5 4 3 1 2 3 4/0

Printed in the U.S.A. 40

First Scholastic trade paperback printing, January 1999

Interior design by Elizabeth B. Parisi

CONTENTS

INTRODUCTION 1
1 DAY-TO-DAY RESISTANCE AND EARLY REVOLTS 11
2 THE MAROONS 25
3 TOUSSAINT LOUVERTURE 41
4 GABRIEL PROSSER 60
5 DENMARK VESEY 71
6 REBEL ABOLITIONISTS 83
7 NAT TURNER 99
8 CINQUE AND THE *AMISTAD* 112
9 HARRIET TUBMAN AND THE UNDERGROUND REBELLION 130
10 JOHN BROWN'S RAID AT HARPERS FERRY 144

EPILOGUE 160
IMPORTANT DATES 166
BIBLIOGRAPHY 172
INDEX 175

AUTHORS' NOTE

Chattel slavery, as it was practiced in the Americas, was a brutal system that reduced human beings to property with no more rights than livestock or household furnishings. This is a book about a few of the men and women, slaves and free blacks, Northerners and Southerners, whites and Native Americans, who became rebels against that system.

For a long while, history dismissed these people as dangerous lunatics and murderers whose logic and wisdom were questionable. Sometimes they were portrayed as people driven to a madness where drastic action seemed the only available course. To some, however, they were heroes and martyrs, worthy of honor and remembrance, because they stood up against one of the vicious forms of human oppression, very often without the slightest chance of ultimate success.

Their rebellious acts, however, served as a constant reminder of the moral and political dangers of slavery. As rebels for a righteous cause, they should be remembered for the terrible risks they knowingly took, the extraordinary determination they displayed, and the important role they played in the abolition of slavery.

We would like to thank all those who helped us complete this project. Our research has taken us from the Caribbean to New England, from Florida to New York, and from the Everglades to Harpers Ferry. We owe a debt of gratitude to all the people who helped us during our visits to historical societies, museums, tour houses, universities, and libraries. We would like to thank our family, especially Moses Andrew McKissack, whose help can't be measured. As always, a special thanks to our editor, Ann Reit.

Patricia and Fredrick McKissack
St. Louis, Missouri
June 1995

A SONG OF REBELLION

ARISE! ARISE! SHAKE OFF YOUR CHAINS
YOUR CAUSE IS JUST SO HEAVEN ORDAINS
TO YOU SHALL FREEDOM BE PROCLAIMED
RAISE YOUR ARMS & BARE YOUR BREASTS,
ALMIGHTY GOD WILL DO THE REST.
BLOW THE CLARION! A WARLIKE BLAST!
CALL EVERY (N)EGRO FROM HIS TASK!
WREST THE SCOURGE FROM BUCKRA'S HAND,
AND DRIVE EACH TYRANT FROM THE LAND.

Blacks along the Sea Island coast of South Carolina developed this song, which expresses their commitment to an armed struggle for freedom.

INTRODUCTION

Slavery is as old as recorded history and so are slave rebellions. Whenever and wherever slavery has existed there has been resistance to it, ranging from individual acts of defiance to well-organized, armed revolts. One historian summarized it even more simply: "The cause of slave revolts is slavery."

Support for that idea can be found on the walls of an ancient Egyptian pyramid. Hieroglyphs show slaves using sabotage, work slow-downs, physical mutilation, and armed rebellion to free themselves from the tyranny of slavery. For centuries the stories of Moses and the Hebrews of ancient Egypt, and Spartacus, who led a slave army against Rome, have served as an inspiration to oppressed people everywhere.

By the time Christopher Columbus, in search of a shorter route to India, stumbled upon a Caribbean island in 1492, which he named San Salvador, slavery was not a new institution and rebellions were not a new response to it.

When the Americas were opened up for European colonization in the sixteenth century, slavery came with it. After taking hold in the Caribbean Islands, slavery spread to North America early in the seventeenth century. Conspiracies and uprisings surfaced almost immediately. On July 26, 1740, the South Carolina Assembly submitted a report to King George II noting that there had been

> *. . . an insurrection of our slaves in which many of the inhabitants were murdered in a barbarous and cruel manner; and that no sooner quelled than another projected in Charles Town, and a third lately in the very heart of the Settlements, but happily discovered in time enough to be prevented.*

Resistance against slavery continued until the Thirteenth Amendment was ratified on December 18, 1865, officially ending slavery on the North American continent. (Slavery in Cuba and Brazil continued until the 1880s.)

For centuries the lie that African people were happy and contented in bondage was accepted as truth. However, a large body of historical data gives us a more accurate picture today. On the huge Caribbean and South American sugarcane plantations slaveholders lived in constant fear of insurrections, and with good reason. First, planters were usually outnumbered by their slaves, and according to historian Eugene D. Genovese, author of *Roll, Jordan, Roll* and other works about slavery, "no people in world history rose in revolt so often or in such numbers or with so large a measure of success," than the slaves of the Americas.

Caribbean and South American slaves rose more often and in larger numbers than those in North America. But rebels of the Old South, such as Cato, reputed leader of the Stono Rebellion, Gabriel Prosser, Denmark Vesey, Nat Turner, the five blacks who fought with John Brown, and others, planned and led rebellions with no less courage or conviction.

Actually, slaveholders panicked at the mere mention of a plot or a conspiracy — real or imagined —

Slaves working on a sugar plantation in the Caribbean during the seventeenth century.

and local and state officials overreacted by trying to suppress all evidence that there had ever been one. It was generally believed, though seldom discussed among whites, that most slaves didn't have the nerve to lead a rebellion, but if one was started, they would have no problem joining it.

In public, people were forbidden to speak the name of a rebel or the revolt he or she led. One eighteenth-century Virginia plantation owner, referring to Nat Turner's revolt of 1831, wrote in his diary, "There was an uprising in Southampton . . . but I dare not speak of it."

Authorities almost always inflated the number of people involved in a conspiracy and insisted upon swift and severe punishment, which sometimes meant many innocent people died. Suspects were rounded up, quickly tried, found guilty, and publicly executed based upon the flimsiest of evidence. In reality, most pre-Civil War revolts were local and involved small numbers of people.

After the authorities had suppressed the rebel movement and the immediate danger had passed, slaveholders pushed for the passage of harsh slave laws, limiting the movement of slaves and terminating what few privileges they had. Following the Stono Rebellion in South Carolina on September 9, 1739, which was much too large to be kept quiet, South Carolina, followed by North Carolina and Virginia, passed a law forbidding blacks to make or have in their possession a drum, because it was considered an "instrument of rebellion." (African drummers could "talk" to each other over great distances.)

During the eighteenth century, the revolutions that took place in France and America set before the world the revolutionary concept that liberty and equality were the rights of all men — not just a privileged few. These ideas were inherently dangerous in slaveholding societies. Motivated by such ideas, Toussaint L'Ouverture led a slave revolution that began in 1791 on the French colony of Saint-Domingue, and ended with the abolition of slavery there and the formation of Haiti, the first black nation in the Western Hemisphere.

Toussaint L'Ouverture's victory over the French was a chilling reminder to North American slaveholders that such an uprising was possible in their own states. In some South Carolina counties where blacks outnumbered whites almost five to one, there was an attempt to keep knowledge of the events in Haiti from filtering into the slave quarters. But, hard as the slave masters tried, nothing could stop the news of Haiti's success from reaching the slaves. Toussaint L'Ouverture's name was spoken with reverence. From city to city, farm to farm, word of his victories was shared in the holes in the ground where blacks held secret "pit schools," in stables, in the fields, in the kitchens, and blacksmith shops. When Haiti's rebel army triumphed over the French, slaves every-

Toussaint L'Ouverture, who wanted to overthrow slavery as a social system.

where found hope in the renewed dream that one day they might live in a world free of slavery.

One master wrote that he feared the "importation of revolution" from the Caribbean, but he failed to recognize that the seeds of rebellion had been planted earlier, in 1776. Blacks had fought for independence in the Continental Army and held their ground at Bunker Hill. Was it so unreasonable, then, that slaves who fought for the lofty ideas set forth in the Declaration of Independence would want to harvest life, liberty, justice, and freedom for themselves and their families, too? And wouldn't they, when denied those basic human rights, take up arms to fight for them, just as their masters had?

The events of the last half of the eighteenth century helped set the stage for the drama leading up to the Civil War. More than a few scholars believe that Gabriel's rebellion of 1800, Denmark Vesey's of 1822, and Nat Turner's of 1831, marked the beginning of a new kind of rebel, one motivated by Toussaint L'Ouverture, the Declaration of Independence, and the French Revolution. Up until then, the goal of most rebels had been to secure freedom from slavery. Toussaint L'Ouverture and Prosser's goal was to overthrow slavery as a social system. Such an idea was frightening to the planter class.

To help protect their slave economy and their privileged way of life, which was increasingly under attack from Northern abolitionists, and to limit the possibilities of future slave revolts, Southern authorities felt it was in their best interest to keep their slaves "profoundly ignorant." By 1850 it was against the law in every Southern state to teach a slave to read and write. (It is interesting to note that many slave owners continued to teach their slaves in spite of the law.) A second more strict Fugitive Slave Law was passed, too, which meant that runaway slaves were no longer safe once they reached a free state. That didn't stop them from running. A rebellious group of otherwise law-abiding people defied the law of the land, and formed a network of escape routes that helped slaves find their way to Canada or Mexico on the Underground Railroad.

As the struggle for the abolition of slavery continued, militant black abolitionists such as David Walker and Henry Highland Garnet became more outspoken about the role free blacks should play in the emancipation of all enslaved people. Both men called for action, even if it meant armed rebellion.

Slaves lived in a hostile and controlled environment, where most of their energy was spent on surviving the harshness of their sunrise to sundown existence. Denied the right to hold meetings or travel about freely made it hard to map out plans. Since most slaves couldn't read or write, all communication had to be conducted verbally, which meant messages and instructions were frequently confused or misinterpreted.

Weapons presented another problem. Slaves had little or no access to guns, and the few knives and axes they were able to secure were no match against the well-armed militias they would have to face. And there was the constant fear of bounty hunters and betrayal.

Some of the earliest revolts were combined efforts between blacks and Native Americans, or poor whites and blacks. Slaveholders soon learned that the "divide and rule" tactic was a very effective way to deter the possibility of rebellion. Poor whites, whose circumstances were not much better than the slaves, were encouraged to feel superior to people of color — whether free or black. From generation to generation, the gap between the two groups widened as racism became more entrenched in American society. For the whites it was far more profitable and less dangerous to catch slaves or serve as overseers than to join them in rebellion.

Runaways also sought allies among Native Americans. Fleeing into Indian Territory, they set up maroon communities, but slavers used specially trained tracking dogs to hunt down their settlements. The slaves called this "being hounded." Slaveholders sponsored the passage of laws that permitted the trading of blankets and skins to the Indians for the return of runaways, and they insisted that fugitive slave clauses be included in all treaties. They encouraged the practice of slavery among the various native groups. Those tribes, such as the Seminoles, who refused to take part in the bounty system found themselves facing the guns of the United States Army, Marines, and Navy, who had come, in part, to get their "property" back by force.

Closer to home, masters promised to free any slave who turned in a rebel, and granted special favors to informants.

A former slave who was interviewed in the 1930s, said, "[Our masters] taught us to be against one another and no matter where you would go you would always find one [slave] that would tattle. . . ." Such bribery worked. Denmark Vesey's and Gabriel Prosser's revolts were betrayed by insiders before they ever happened.

It is no wonder that Harriet Tubman said, "I kept my eyes on the target, trusting no one but God and my wits. I never took time to study on what I was doing," because if she had, she might never have escaped and then been able to return to rescue others. "I just did what I had to do," she said. And basically this is what all rebels did.

This book will not address every American slave rebel or revolutionary action. That would take volumes. We will not detail all the rebellions of the Caribbean Islands and South America, for they were myriad, but we will highlight Haiti's Toussaint L'Ouverture and the African rebel Cinque, because of the impact their revolts had on the rebels of the Old South and the abolitionist movement in general.

The leaders we have chosen were all people of courage and purpose, totally committed to their cause, and motivated by the highest of principals. They were human beings, with strengths and weaknesses, failures and successes. With rare exception most of these rebels knew that for them the complete abolition of slavery was a non-negotiable issue between their masters and themselves. The only course of action they believed open to them was to end their enslavement by force. Sadly for all involved, in the end, force is what it took.

1

DAY-TO-DAY RESISTANCE AND EARLY REVOLTS

During the sixteenth century, the New World opened for European colonization. The Caribbean Islands' hot, humid climate and rich soil combined to create excellent growing conditions for sugarcane. Gradually, it became established among the European powers that slave labor would be used to do the backbreaking work that was required to grow and process sugarcane profitably. At first, the colonists tried to enslave the indigenous people they found living there, but the planters ran into a wall of resistance. The Indians (as they were misnamed by Columbus when he believed he had reached India) ran away into the mountains or died from disease and exhaustion. Then the importation of African slaves became a viable alternative. Slavery was well-established in Africa and the Middle East. Arab dealers in cooperation with warring African kings provided a steady supply of captives for the European slave market.

Massive numbers of blacks were taken from West Africa and brought to the Caribbean to work in the sugarcane fields. They were worked until they

Slaves cultivating sugarcane on a large plantation in the West Indies.

dropped dead from exhaustion, ran away into the mountains, or revolted. Planters wasted little time looking for fugitives, because there was usually a shipload of fresh workers waiting in the harbor. However, the planters were always concerned about revolts, so any hint of the rebel spirit was dealt with swiftly and severely. But the system kept spawning one rebel after another.

Slave revolts seemed to have occurred more frequently in areas where there was a high ratio of blacks to whites, and slaves to free men, such as Jamaica, Saint-Domingue (Haiti), Brazil, and British Guyana.

A slaver noted in his log, "Every part of the world where domestic slavery is established, may be occasionally liable to insurrection and disquiet, more especially where the slaves constitute the majority of the inhabitants."

Slave uprisings are a matter of record all over the Caribbean, Mexico, and South America. The first large-scale revolt of African slaves took place on the plantation of Christopher Columbus's son, Diego, in 1522 on the island of Hispaniola. As early as 1546, slaves mounted a significant revolt in Mexico. There were several others in Venezuela between 1552 and 1556.

Slavery as it was practiced in the Caribbean and South America served as a model for North American slavery. Slavers boasted that Africans coming from the Caribbean had been "broken in" at "seasoning" stations. But as Genovese noted: "Because a high proportion of seasoned Africans . . . in some cases, were involved in plots and revolts, they also served as models for slave resistance in North America."

Slavery officially began in the North American British colonies in August 1619, when a Dutch vessel, coming from the Caribbean, brought twenty black indentured servants into Jamestown, Virginia. That same year, the Virginia House of Burgesses had met in Jamestown and approved indentured servitude. Thereafter, white and black indentured servants were traded there and in other major slave markets, such as Charleston (South Carolina) and New Amsterdam (New York).

According to the law of that day, indentured servants worked for a period, on average, of seven years, then they were freed with full rights of citizenship. But as the plantations expanded and the demand for laborers increased, the enslavement of Africans was legalized, first in Massachusetts in 1641, followed by Connecticut in 1650, Virginia in 1661, Maryland in 1663, New York and New Jersey in 1664, South Carolina in 1682; Rhode Island and Pennsylvania in 1700, North Carolina in 1715, and Georgia in 1750.

The first serious slave conspiracy in colonial America was in Gloucester County, Virginia, in 1663, when white indentured servants and slaves plotted to overthrow their masters and make good their escape into the wilderness. Their plot was exposed by an informer, and they were punished in the usual way — by death, beatings, or brandings. After this and several other cooperative incidents, slave masters quickly realized they couldn't allow white indentured servants and slaves to become allies. So every effort was made to keep the two groups separate and in conflict.

A series of slave laws was adopted, restricting the rights of slaves and free blacks. One law, passed in 1664, forbade interracial marriages between blacks and English women. This law stayed on the books of some states until the early 1970s.

By the mid-eighteenth century, chattel slavery was widely practiced throughout North America. Chattel means property. Blacks were owned by their masters. They could be bought and sold in total disregard and denial of their humanity, and with no likelihood of freedom for themselves or their children. According to several historians, the slavery that evolved in the colonies was "designed for maximum economic gain," and supported by the "belief in and the argument for the inherent inferiority of Africans because of color and physical type." Race and racism

An 1884 wood engraving showing African captives.

provided the excuse slaveowners needed to allow themselves to own slaves without feeling guilty.

Periodically the chains that bound a race of people were strengthened by the passage of additional slave codes. Carolina, which later separated into North and South Carolina, enacted one of the most stringent set of laws governing slaves to be found anywhere in the New World. Owners were warned against excessive cruelty because that led to revolts. Yet, the hours for working slaves were set at no more than fifteen hours per day between March 25 and September 25, and no more than fourteen hours between September 25 and March 25. That translated from "can to can't" in slave language — which meant from "can see in the morning to can't see at night."

Georgia's slave code, adopted in 1755, was taken from South Carolina's. The selling of liquor to slaves was forbidden. Seven blacks "being out together constituted a mob," and masters were encouraged not to teach their slaves how to read and write. Laws were easily written but hard to enforce. Some slave masters resented being told how to treat their "property," and disregarded the laws and ran their plantations as they pleased.

When it became clear that chattel slavery was replacing the indentured system, resistance increased. In 1688, a group of Pennsylvania Quakers were the first whites to protest slavery in an official written document. But even before then, blacks never ceased in their desire or demands to be free. Some chose a more covert form of resistance on a day-to-day basis. These "quiet rebels," used sabotage, work slow-downs, and faked illness to undermine day-to-day order and routine.

Craftsmen who knew their value to their masters, and new arrivals from Africa, were among the most defiant. Since they gained nothing from their own hard work, they used every opportunity available to strike at the system.

Slaves with a rebellious nature were feared for they set examples for others, but that still didn't break their spirit. Masters were constantly plagued with tools that were mysteriously broken, gates that were left open for livestock to stray, boats left to drift, and false illnesses. All of this cost the planters time and money. One slaveholder wrote about his slaves: "I'm nearly worried to death with them — if I had a jail, I should lock them up every night."

In the Big House, trusted servants pretended to be slow and stupid around their masters, who, in turn, talked freely in front of them. In reality the slaves were eavesdropping, then taking information back to the quarters.

The communication network among slaves was amazing. They used songs, stories, and coded language to confuse and bewilder their masters who never really understood how it was done. To them a singing slave was happy; they had no idea that a song could be just a song, but then again, it could be a signal to a runaway. And it was all happening right under the masters' noses.

Some slaveholders countered this kind of rebellion in different ways. Some applied pressure by hiring ruthless overseers who beat work out of their slaves; some masters used threats or paternalistic kindness and a few comforts to guarantee loyalty and compliance; still others used bribery, such as the promise of freedom in exchange for hard work.

From generation to generation slave children were taught that they were inferior beings meant to be servants, and white children were taught that they were superior to all others. In time, large numbers within each group came to believe what they'd been taught. On any plantation there were more than a few slaves who were loyal and faithful to their masters or afraid to disobey them. But there were always a few — and current research shows the number was much larger than ever expected — who stubbornly refused to relinquish their right to be free, and no amount of coercion or kindness could change them.

Some of these people took more immediate action against the system. One slave, Randall, for example, had angered the overseer, who ordered three blacks to hold Randall while he beat him. Randall spoke to his fellow slaves: "Boys, you all know me; you know that I can handle any three of you, and the man that lays hands on me shall die. This white man can't whip me himself, and therefore he has called you to help him." The overseer was unable to prevail upon them to seize and secure Randall, and finally ordered them all to go to their work together. When slaves were too valuable to kill or sell, they were labeled "crazy."

In another documented case, a woman who was being sold away from her family, pretended to be blind. When nobody would buy her, her master took her back home. She got a terrible beating, but she was allowed to stay with her family.

One master got the surprise of his life when his own slave sold him! This master took his very light-skinned black to the marketplace to be sold. Meanwhile he went to make arrangements for a hotel room. When the master returned he was bound in chains. While he was trying to prove that he wasn't a mulatto attempting to pass himself off as a white man, the real slave escaped.

Rather than live in slavery, some people chose more destructive forms of rebellion, such as murder and suicide. For example, there are instances of slave mothers, driven mad by the grief of having their children sold away from them, taking the lives of their newborns and sometimes killing themselves.

The story of Ebo Landing on Sea Island off the coast of Georgia reminds us of the extremes to which people will go to be free. A group of African men, women, and children committed mass suicide by walking into the water. According to the legend that

A rebellion on board a slave ship; slaves are seen jumping overboard.

developed around the event, in their deaths they flew away to their homeland — free and unfettered. Slaves also used self-mutilation, escape, and arson to lash out at the slave system.

Armed revolts were the most aggressive forms of resistance, and the least talked about. Most uprisings, prior to 1800, began as spontaneous acts of desperation — in response to a brutal beating, the selling of a spouse, or the sudden withdrawal of a privilege. Sometimes a leader emerged out of this immediate conflict and rallied dissident slaves from neighboring plantations. Without weapons or a plan, however, many of these revolts were short-lived and soon fizzled out, especially when the local militia captured or killed the leader.

Some of the earliest slave rebellions occurred in the Northern colonies. In 1638, Boston experienced a minor uprising, and in New York there was a major revolt in 1712.

By 1706 the black population in New York was a little over 2,100 in a total population of 18,000, yet the colony enacted slave codes stating that "Baptism did not provide grounds for a claim to freedom; no slave could be a witness against a freeman; runaways found forty miles north of Albany could be killed if witnessed by two credible white men, and all blacks — free or slave — could not be in the streets after nightfall without a lantern with a lighted candle in it."

On April 7, 1712, twenty-seven armed slaves met in an orchard near the center of the city. They set fire to an outhouse and, as the whites came to extinguish the fire, they shot at them. Nine whites were killed before the militia was able to put down the revolt. The men were quickly tried, convicted, and executed in various ways, ranging from public burning to starvation. New Yorkers reacted by adding extremely rigid slave codes on the record books.

In 1723, there was another group of fires set in Boston, which led people to believe a slave plot was behind it. The local militia was ordered to police the slaves. Another plot was reported in Burlington, Pennsylvania, in 1734. Then, in 1741, another conspiracy was suspected in New York. Several buildings were destroyed by fire, which set off a wave of hysteria that resulted in the deaths of people who might have been innocent. Although there are existing "confessions" given by the condemned conspirators as they hung on the scaffold, they can hardly be accepted as reliable evidence of a conspiracy. When the smoke cleared, the mob dispersed, and all the anger vented, twenty-nine blacks had been hanged or burned alive, along with four white men, and two white women.

The burnings in New York may or may not have been part of a plot, but records indicate that there were other slave plots throughout the colonies between 1660 and 1760. The most serious one took place at Stono, South Carolina, led by an Angolan slave named Cato. (Some sources refer to him as Jemmy.)

On September 9, 1739, Cato used his knowledge of drums to "speak" to other African-born slaves, and before long a group of twenty men and women had come together as a rebel fighting unit. Beginning at the Stono River, about twenty miles west of Charleston, Cato overtook two guards and captured the arms and ammunition in the storehouse. Then the rebels marched south toward Florida, where they

Site of the Stono Rebellion, which took place on September 9, 1739.

planned to live alongside other runaways. As they marched they beat their drums to attract other slaves to their cause, and anybody who tried to stop them was killed.

The army of about one hundred marched about 12 miles. But then Cato did a strange thing. He stopped in a clearing to celebrate their victory; sadly, it was premature. This delay gave their masters time to organize the militia and pursue them. Cato and his men were surrounded. Over the next ten days, 14 slaves and half that many whites were killed. In the end

Cato and the others were captured and executed immediately.

One of the most costly drains on the plantation society was the runaway, the choice that thousands of slaves chose. Many runaways formed their own communities in swamps, forests, and mountains. They were known as *maroons*.

2

THE MAROONS

The term maroon is believed to be a derivative of the Spanish word *cimarrón,* which refers to domestic animals that have escaped and gone wild. The word was first used in the Caribbean with reference to runaways who organized themselves into communities that were located in hard-to-reach but easy-to-defend areas.

One of the earliest maroon societies in the New World was formed in 1663 when planters in Dutch and French Guyana, South America, sent their slaves into the forest to avoid paying taxes on them. After the tax assessors left, the slaves refused to return to their masters. They remained in the interior and set up their own "nations." From their strongholds, they resisted being captured and conducted long-term guerrilla warfare against the colonial plantations.

One of the strongest of these rebels was an African-born slave named Cudjoe (Cujo, Kudjo) who claimed that he was of the Akan people of Ghana.

In 1725 Cudjoe led a band of runaways into the Jamaican mountains where they established their own state. After years of costly struggle, the British governor was forced to sign a treaty with Cudjoe in 1738. Cudjoe agreed to send back any runaway slaves in return for rights of self-government and a tax-free existence.

It seems unreasonable that a man who fought so hard for his own freedom would send another person back into slavery. To help understand his decision, it is necessary to understand his culture. Cudjoe grew up in West Africa where owning slaves was an accepted institution, with long-standing customs and traditions. In Mali, for example, slaves could practice their own religion, communicate in their own language, marry a person from their own culture (or sometimes from the master's family). Some slaves could rise to positions of authority within their master's house or become valued counselors or advisors to him. At one time, if a slave was freed, it was not uncommon for him or her to become a slaveholder. There was no shame attached to being a slave. In fact the shame was directed at the masters of runaways.

Cudjoe's purpose in running away was not to end slavery as an institution but to guarantee personal freedom for himself and his followers. That was where his loyalties were focused. Other groups were expected to fend for themselves and their own people.

As fragmented as they were, the maroon populations of South America and the Caribbean were a constant drain on colonial resources. The Portuguese couldn't stop the holdouts of Brazil nor could the Spanish in Cuba. In fact, maroon resistance was so strong, several European powers signed treaties with maroon rebels. The terms of these agreements were similar to those negotiated with Cudjoe: Each group was guaranteed its autonomy in exchange for cooperation in returning fugitive slaves.

During the seventeenth century, slaves who came to the colonies from the islands brought with them the knowledge of how maroon societies operated, and some of them helped form the first runaway communities in North America. Some of these first

"A Rebel Negro," artist unknown.

groups included white indentured servants and Native Americans, as well as blacks. There are references to maroon communities being established in the mountains of North Carolina, Virginia, and in the swamps of Florida and Georgia. The Great Dismal Swamp, an area covering thirty by fifteen miles along the Virginia and North Carolina border, was a favorite hideout for runaways.

Life in a maroon camp was as harsh as the surroundings. Octave Johnson, a twenty-one-year-old runaway, joined a band of maroons outside New Orleans where it was reported there were three hundred fugitives living in the swamps. Johnson described his life among the maroons to a Union Army officer during the Civil War:

> *I had to steal my food; took turkeys, chickens, and pigs; before I left our number had increased to thirty, of whom ten were women; we were four miles behind the plantation house; sometimes we would rope the beef cattle and drag them to our hiding place; we obtained matches from our friends on the plantation; we slept on logs and burned cypress leaves to make a smoke and keep away mosquitoes; Eugene Jardeau, master of hounds, hunted for us for three months; often those at work would betray those in the swamp for fear of being implicated in their escape; we furnished meat to our*

> *fellow-servants in the field, who would return corn meal. . . .*

As early as 1670, Virginia set out to destroy all known maroon settlements before they posed a threat to plantation safety. To do this they sought help from the Native Americans who lived in the area.

Colonial slaveholders feared an alliance between Native American and black runaways, and resented the adoption of blacks into their group. Early Carolina documents are filled "with dread of an Afro-Indian collaboration." Gary B. Nash wrote in *Red, White, and Black:*

> *By fashioning the harshest slave code of any of the colonies, by paying dearly for Indian support at critical moments, and by militarizing their society, white Carolinians were able to restrict the flow of blacks into the back country. The Cherokee hill country never became the equivalent of the Maroon hideaways in Jamaica or the Brazilian quilombos as a refuge for runaway slaves as many Carolinians feared.*

Maroon communities were never as successful as they might have been, because colonists took measures to keep the blacks and Indians divided, first by using fear and ignorance and then by playing one group against the other. Indians were encouraged to become slaveholders, which many of them did. The Cherokee, Chickasaw, Choktaw, and Creek owned slaves but, much to the dissatisfaction of Southern planters, slavery was practiced more like a fairly managed sharecropping system.

All treaties between the colonist and Native American groups contained a "fugitive slave clause," and Indians were often used to track and lead colonists to maroon villages. Conversely, in times of conflict, some blacks were given their freedom for fighting with whites in wars against Indians. According to Genovese: "Effective white manipulation of Indians and blacks against each other reduced possibilities for the organization of stable maroon colonies."

But, in spite of these efforts, in the early nineteenth century Southerners' worst fears were realized when maroon activity shifted to Florida. The Seminoles and runaway blacks formed a major alliance which by its very existence was considered an "outrage" to Georgians.

Spanish-controlled Florida had been a haven for runaway blacks for several decades. In 1750, a group of Creek Indians left Georgia because of tribal disputes and migrated to Florida, too. Creeks began calling this group Seminoles, which in the Creek language means runaways. The two peoples of color prospered in peaceful, cooperative communities. Their relationship with each other was based on the integrity of the individual and mutual group respect. Blacks brought their knowledge of rice cultivation, and the Seminoles shared their land. The partnership yielded a prosperous economy because everybody had a vested interest in the success of their individual endeavors.

The Seminoles adopted black men and women into their group, and marriages between blacks and Seminoles were commonplace. Before long a black-Seminole population developed.

Colonial Georgia complained loudly about the runaway problem, and blatantly disregarded Spanish borders by sending Georgia militia into Florida in search of runaways, but Seminole and black warriors repeatedly drove them back. After the Revolutionary War, there was a push to annex Florida, but public opinion was against the move, so the idea died from lack of support.

There was a fort located on the Apalachicola River in the Florida Panhandle not fifty miles from Georgia. When the British withdrew, after the War of 1812, it was handed over to a group of black Seminoles. Known as Fort Negro, it was commanded by a part-black, part-Seminole named Garcia.

Described as a lean, tense-looking man, Garcia was respected for his courage as a warrior, but feared because of his cruelty to enemies. He was a strong leader, and the perfect man to put in charge of defending the fort. On May 16, 1816, General Andrew

The black Seminole survivors of Fort Negro were forced into slavery.

Jackson, the hero of the War of 1812, ordered General Edmund Pendleton Gaines, commander of the Southern Frontier, to blow up the fort, "regardless of the ground on which it stands . . . and restore all stolen Negroes to their rightful owners."

In July 1816, United States armed forces, aided by two offshore navy gunboats, stood outside Fort Negro. Garcia's men raised the British flag as a challenge. They were refusing to surrender. Garcia fired a cannon shot to emphasize his point. Both sides exchanged a number of cannonballs. Then one volley landed in the fort's ammunition storage area, and the place went up in flames and smoke. As the gunpowder exploded, over two hundred people were killed and sixty-four wounded. Garcia was captured and executed.

A few families fled into the swamps and hid in the tall grasses. Those who survived were sent back to slavery, even though they had been born in Florida and had never been slaves. But it was all perfectly legal, because according to slave laws a black person who did not have papers stating that he or she was free, could be captured and sold.

In January 1818, Jackson, with two mounted regiments, captured Pensacola, and in 1819 the United States paid Spain five million dollars for Florida, to help soften Jackson's renegade actions. By 1821, without declaring war, Florida passed into United States hands.

Whites were clamoring to move into Florida, but they demanded safety. Something had to be done about the Indians and the black runaways.

Jackson was sympathetic to slaveholders because he owned slaves himself, and in his opinion, "Indians were savages who stood in the way of progress."

The United States government decided that Native Americans had to live on a reservation in the south-central part of the state. This swampy and inhospitable land, known as the Everglades, was very different from northern Florida where the Seminoles had raised crops and fruit. Yet, in 1823, Seminoles agreed to move to the reservation. A young Seminole leader whose name was Asi-yaholo, or Black Drink Crier, watched in horror as his people were driven from their land, and black friends and family were taken against their will. He spoke out against the treatment of his people — both black and Indian.

United States policy tried to undermine the strong friendship between blacks and Seminoles. But the council leaders would not condone slavery. To get around the government, they began buying members of their family and then freeing them. This further angered government agents. Some Seminole leaders argued that it was better to allow the whites to take the blacks than to jeopardize their families by trying to protect them. This argument didn't hold up, because so many Seminoles were racially mixed. Who was black? Who was Indian?

Asi-yaholo was one who was against the re-enslavement of free blacks. By then he was a vocal leader among the Seminoles, highly respected by his peers. When whites spoke his name it sounded like Osceola, and that is how he became known.

In 1829, Andrew Jackson was elected President of the United States. His administration is remembered for being one of the harshest toward Native Americans. "Old Hickory," as Jackson was nicknamed, wanted all Native American groups to move west of the Mississippi River. The Indian Removal Act put into law one of the most shameful events in American

Osceola, Seminole leader, refused to turn black allies over to slaveholders.

history, the forced resettlement of Native Americans to reservations often far removed from their traditional homelands. The Seminoles were one of the five Native American groups that were affected by the policy. Contrary to all prior treaties, the Seminoles were once again expected to leave their farms and this time move hundreds of miles away to Oklahoma, Indian Territory.

In June 1832, Osceola refused to agree to leave his lands and home. He was prepared to resist to the death. Some Seminoles left Florida and moved to Oklahoma, but those who refused to go rallied around Osceola.

First, Osceola had a personal vendetta to settle. He killed Wiley Thompson, an Indian agent who had forced Osceola at gunpoint while being held in prison, to sign a treaty agreeing to leave Florida. In December 1835, Seminoles scored a victory when they defeated Major Francis Dade's entire relief force. President Jackson was furious.

General Winfield Scott was given command of the army in Florida, but his tactics were no match for the hit-and-run guerrilla tactics of Osceola's men. Dissatisfied, Jackson replaced Scott with General Sidney Thomas Jesup who was told to use any means necessary to defeat the Seminoles.

Osceola's people were tired and hungry. Constantly on the run, they had been unable to plant and harvest crops. Osceola was against the wall, but he refused to give in especially regarding slavery.

In May 1837, General Jesup sent a message to Osceola, asking for a meeting. Weary and ill, Osceola agreed. More than 3,000 Seminoles of every size and hue showed up at Fort Brooke at Tampa Bay. Osceola spoke eloquently on behalf of his people. Jesup insisted that the Seminoles had to migrate to the West. When pinned to specifics, the Seminoles realized that they would be settled among their old Indian enemies. Slaveholders in Florida and Georgia insisted that blacks were *their* property and refused to permit them to leave with the Seminoles. Osceola leaped to his feet. "These black people have lived with us for many years. They are friends and allies. We will not turn them over to the whites."

The line had been drawn. Osceola and his people fought on. The order came from Washington: ". . . break the resistance."

In October 1837, Osceola agreed with a number of other leaders, under the white flag of truce, to meet with General Joseph Hernandez of the Florida militia near the city of St. Augustine. Suddenly, Osceola was seized by soldiers, beaten, and tied up. The truce had been a trick to capture him and his men.

Under heavy guard, Osceola was moved to Fort Moultrie, South Carolina. When word of how he had been captured spread among the American people, they were ashamed. "Is this a country without honor?" one editorial asked. Taking a person captive under a white flag was considered the highest form of cowardice. A "free Osceola" drive began. But it was too late. Osceola, weakened by malaria and fatigue, died in January 1838. He was not yet thirty-five.

Back in Florida, the war was far from over. The Seminoles fought on. When Osceola had been taken under the white flag, so had one of his captains, a leader named Wild Cat. While being held at Fort Marion, Wild Cat and his men fasted to lose weight, then loosened the bars on the windows and slipped away in the middle of the night.

Deep in the swamps, Wild Cat called a meeting of the warriors who had fought with Osceola. Among them were two black Seminoles, Negro Abraham and John Horse, who pledged their allegiance to Wild Cat. John Horse, considered a shrewd negotiator and a skilled warrior, soon became second in command. Together the two men led militant Seminole forces that refused to leave their homes.

The Seminoles knew their land and loved it. Abundant with life, the swamps and marshes of the Everglades provided food and shelter for them. Living on the run, the Seminoles moved among the cypress trees with speed and agility. Many of the United States soldiers who came there weren't prepared for what they encountered in the Florida swamps —

Negro Abraham, a black Seminole warrior.

snakes, alligators, oppressive heat, and mosquitoes.

By 1843, the climate and the endless struggle had taken its toll on both the soldiers and the Seminoles. Most of the Seminole Nation, including five hundred blacks who were finally allowed to migrate with them, had reached Indian Territory in Oklahoma. Still there were hold-outs who refused to leave.

The U.S. government finally realized that the Seminole Wars were costly, too costly to continue. The government had spent millions of dollars and 1,500 soldiers had lost their lives. The death toll among the Seminoles and their black allies, who were force-marched across the country, was staggering. At last, the war ended in 1843 when troops were withdrawn.

Yet the United States could not claim a victory.

There were still Seminoles who would not migrate West. The black and Native American descendants of runaway slaves and defiant Indians still live in Florida today. They are proud members of the Seminole Nation, the only Native Americans who never surrendered. The name Seminole became synonymous with bravery and unbeatable spirit.

3

TOUSSAINT LOUVERTURE

The country we know today as Haiti was at one time the French colony of Saint-Domingue. Located on the island of Hispaniola, it was the place where Christopher Columbus established his first settlement in the New World. After many years of Spanish rule that saw the destruction of the native islanders and the beginning of African slavery, French settlers occupied the western end of the island and, in 1697, it was formally recognized as Saint-Domingue. The colony was small, about the size of Maryland, and much of the area consisted of mountains. In the langauge of the native Taino Indians "Haiti" meant "mountainous land."

Within one hundred years, Saint-Domingue became the richest colony in the Caribbean. By 1791 there were 35,000 white residents in the colony, but there were at least 500,000 slaves, most of whom worked on plantations where sugarcane, cotton, coffee, and indigo were grown. There was another group called mulattoes or "people of color." These were the descendants of European men and African slave women. It was customary for mulattoes to be given their freedom and a parcel of land when they reached age twenty-one. By 1789 their numbers had reached 30,000 and as a separate class they had grown prosperous. They owned at least a quarter of the land and as many as a third of the slaves.

There were few, if any, places where the practice of slavery was as cruel and inhumane as Saint-Domingue. Men and women were beaten, branded, maimed, and killed, often in ways that only the most depraved mind could imagine. Many slaves ran away to the mountains where they lived as maroons in

The Night of Fire, Saint-Domingue, August 22, 1791.

isolated spots beyond the reach of a special colonial slave patrol, staffed only by mulattoes.

On August 22, 1791, after careful and secret planning by slave leaders in a place called Alligator Woods, an enormous slave rebellion started. Slaves on five plantations rose up and killed the owners and overseers, setting fire to anything that would burn. Within a matter of hours the fires spread across the plains and thousands of other slaves had joined the uprising. The next morning there was a gigantic wall of fire and smoke that could be seen from distant islands. Before it was over, 900 plantations — buildings, fields, and crops — had been reduced to ashes. Avenging themselves for years of abuse, the slaves massacred thousands of whites and mulattoes. Those who could, escaped to the port city, Cap François.

One of the persons whose life was disrupted by the Night of Fire was Toussaint L'Ouverture, a slave who had lived all his life at Breda plantation, about fifteen miles from the capital. He was forty-seven years old, and in comparison to other slaves on the island, he had enjoyed a good and comfortable life. Breda was most unusual in that the owner treated the slaves with a degree of compassion and kindness that was known throughout the colony.

Born on May 2, 1743, which was then the Feast of All Saints (*Tous Saints,* in French), he was named François Dominique Toussaint. His father, brought as a slave from Africa, enjoyed special treatment because of his talent and demeanor. He was given his own plot of land and was allowed to marry, something that slaves were rarely permitted to do in Saint-Domingue.

As a boy, Toussaint Breda, as he was called then, was sickly and thin as a stick. In fact, those around him at the time had given him a nickname that meant "fragile stick." His health improved gradually and by the time he reached adolescence he could outdo his friends in endurance and stamina. He was an excellent swimmer and had a special fondness for horses. Riding frequently across the fields of the plantation, he was called the centaur of the plains. People were amazed at his ability to make horses follow his commands. He enjoyed working in the stables and learned to take care of the horses when they were hurt or sick.

One of the most fortunate things that happened to Toussaint was that he was encouraged to learn to read and write, something very much discouraged by the colonial administrators. His teacher was a Roman Catholic priest named Simon Baptiste, who also shared his knowledge of plants and herbs with his young pupil. Toussaint was raised from birth as a Roman Catholic and from Father Baptiste he received his instruction in religion, which included a knowledge of Latin. The plantation manager and his wife were particularly impressed with the young boy's intelligence. They allowed him to borrow books from the plantation library. He had a special fondness for books about famous people in history. It is said that he enjoyed the story of Spartacus, a slave who led a large rebellion of slaves against Rome. One day Toussaint himself would be known as the "black Spartacus."

As a young adult, Toussaint supervised the household staff at the plantation. He also became the official coachman, taking the manager and others to the capital and other places around the district. As the coachman, he obtained a much wider view of the world of Saint-Domingue, including the urban life of the capital.

In his early thirties, Toussaint married Suzanne Simon, a slave on the plantation who already had a mulatto child. They had two other children. On Sundays the family attended Mass together and worked in the garden on the tract of land that had been given to him. Toussaint was greatly admired by other slaves on the plantation: He could read and write; he knew the outside world of the whites; as a supervisor he was kind and fair; and when they were ill, he used his knowledge of medicinal herbs and his skill as a "horse doctor" to heal their aches and pains. From all appearances, Toussaint Breda, respected by the whites and blacks, led what he himself called "a peaceful and comfortable life."

But the fires of August 1791 changed everything. Knowing that it would be only hours before the revolt swept through Breda, Toussaint first arranged to have his wife and children taken over the border into the neighboring colony of Santo Domingo. Then he took the plantation manager's wife north to Cap François. She and her husband soon left for the United States. On his return, he found everything in ashes. Most of the slaves had left. The place where he had lived all his life no longer existed. He was now homeless.

With everything in ruins, Toussaint decided to make his way to the army of rebel slaves. When he reached them, he discovered that his services were much needed. Appointed physician in chief of the army, he busied himself by healing sick and wounded rebel slaves. His talents made him valuable for other reasons. One of the very few slaves who could read, Toussaint was chosen to be military secretary to Biassou, one of the leaders of the rebellion. Within months he was put in charge of his own band of men.

From his readings of Julius Caesar and other famous military leaders, Toussaint had acquired a basic knowledge about the tactics and strategies of warfare. Using this knowledge and his common sense, he proceeded to put his recruits through a rigorous regimen of training and preparation. Although most lacked proper clothing and shoes, they learned to march in formation, to crawl unnoticed through the woods, to fight, and to shoot. Above all, they learned to follow

Toussaint Louverture, the Father of Haiti.

orders. Following Toussaint was not hard; they trusted him and had confidence that he knew what he was doing. He had studied the whites and could anticipate their actions. He could ride a horse better than anyone else — and longer, too. He was their doctor — a father image, known affectionately as Wise Toussaint, Papa Toussaint, Old Toussaint.

As the French colonial troops and civilian volunteers moved inland to regain control of the colony, the rebel army headed east over the border into Spanish Santo Domingo where they found refuge and assistance. Spain, which was readying itself for a war with France, found it very convenient to promote disorder. By helping the slaves to fight the French soldiers, it would be easier for Spanish soldiers to come in and take possession of the colony. The rebel leaders received commissions as officers of the army of the king of Spain. Jean François and Biassou were named generals. Toussaint was now a colonel. While in Santo Domingo he saw his family and continued preparing his troops for the day when they would invade Saint-Domingue as Spanish soldiers. Before leaving he wrote a public letter to the slaves:

Brothers and Friends:

I am Toussaint L'Ouverture. My name is perhaps known to you. I am bent on vengeance. I desire the establishment of Liberty and

Equality in Saint-Domingue. I am working to achieve this aim. Unite with us, brothers, and fight with us for the same cause.

Your most obedient and humble servant.

TOUSSAINT L'OUVERTURE

This was the first time that he used the name L'Ouverture in his correspondence. (Later he changed the spelling to Louverture, omitting the apostrophe.) The French word, *l'ouverture,* means "the opening." Some historians of the time have said that the French gave him the name, either because he had lost his front teeth and had a wide gap or opening there, or because whenever the French soldiers thought they had him surrounded, he always found an opening in their lines. Toussaint said that he added it simply because he thought it was a nice name.

In August 1793, the Spanish colonel now led his men back over the border to fight the French soldiers of General Laveaux. Things did not go well at first, but soon the long hours of preparation began to pay off as French regiments were routed in battle after battle. The black regiments cut a path from the eastern border across to Gonaives, an important town on the western coast. Now the French soldiers in the south could not reach those in the north. It was a major achievement, one that made it possible for regular Spanish soldiers to capture the northern half of Saint-Domingue for Spain. It might have happened, except for a change of policy in Paris and a change of heart by Toussaint.

For five years the changing governments of France had squabbled over the civil rights of nonwhites. At first the concern was only for the mulattoes whose representatives pressed hard for equality as citizens of France. Neither the colonial whites nor the mulattoes favored freedom for the slaves. In the summer of 1793, however, Léger Sonthonax, the French commissioner in Saint-Domingue, granted freedom and French citizenship to hundreds of black fighters who came to his aid in a bitter battle with whites and mulattoes in Cap François. Later he extended the grant of freedom to all slaves in the north. Following up on this action, the legislature in Paris abolished slavery in all of its colonies on February 3, 1794.

The abolition of slavery was the thing Toussaint most coveted. He knew that the Spanish and the British had no such intention, but rather that they planned to conquer the colony and put the slaves back to work. After secret negotiations with General Laveaux, Toussaint made the decision to turn his back on his Spanish allies and join the side of the French. To the Spaniards, Toussaint was a traitor; to the French, he was a hero and savior. For Toussaint himself, loyalty to the cause of freedom was his first duty.

After changing sides, Toussaint, now a general,

teamed up with General Laveaux to drive the Spanish out of the colony. While going about this task, he used every opportunity to encourage all the ex-slaves to return to work as cultivators and farmers to raise food for the colony and crops for export. Among the various leaders in the colony, Toussaint was alone in dreaming and planning for a new society not based on slavery, in which blacks, mulattoes, and whites worked for a common good and a prosperity shared by all. His hopes for such a Saint-Domingue could be seen in his earlier campaign when he took special care that the white planters were not robbed or unnecessarily harmed.

With conditions in the north now under control, Toussaint marched south where Laveaux was taking on a large expeditionary force of British soldiers. Mulattoes, led by André Rigaud and others, had formed their own regiments to fight the British. For Toussaint this was a war with strange allies. White French planters had gone over to the side of the king of England in the hope of maintaining slavery and subduing the mulattoes. The mulattoes, while fighting for France, hated all whites as a group, and were equally determined to hold on to their slaves. As the war raged on, Toussaint's soldiers, many now seasoned veterans, attacked British defenses and gradually forced them back into the coastal towns.

The British had other problems. Yellow fever and malaria, diseases for which people who grew up on the island had developed some immunity, struck the newly arriving soldiers and sailors like a great plague. Thousands died within months of their arrival. Between the casualties suffered on the battlefield and those lost to yellow fever and malaria, the British commander, General Thomas Maitland, finally had to admit defeat and negotiate with Toussaint to remove his remaining troops. In a final effort to undermine the French, Maitland urged Toussaint to declare himself king of Haiti.

Now victorious over Spain and Great Britain, the man who was once called "fragile stick" looked more and more like the "Black Spartacus." By this time he was lieutenant governor as well as second in command of all French forces. Yet for all of his success in war, what Toussaint wanted most was peace and the chance to build the multiracial society of his dreams. He invited white planters to return and restart the plantations, this time not with slaves but with paid cultivators. Many did return. But his efforts were thwarted by the French commissioners who for different reasons continued to inflame racial hatred in the colony. Sonthonax despised the white planters and the mulattoes. He had once written: "Saint-Domingue should belong to the blacks. They have earned it by their sweat." His successor was Gabriel Hédouville, a man representing the fears and jealousy of Napoleon Bonaparte. Hédouville arrived with specific instructions to undermine Toussaint by fostering the long-festering hatred that the mulattoes felt toward the former slaves. In the case of both of these officials, Toussaint masterminded threats of mob violence to force their departures, but not before they succeeded in setting the stage for a civil war.

In June 1799, General Rigaud attacked a town of white planters whom Toussaint had invited to return. This was quickly followed by uprisings of mulattoes throughout the colony. It seemed a desperate and insane attempt to gain power by killing all the whites and blacks. This time Toussaint responded with anger and vengeance. Instructing his officers to retaliate with great severity, he sent his most dreaded officer, Jean-Jacques Dessalines, to subdue the mulatto stronghold in the southern half of Saint-Domingue. The fighting was vicious and intense. It became known as the War of the Knives because the combatants used knives, picks, and every other tool they could get their hands on to inflict wounds. Dessalines showed no mercy as he massacred every mulatto he found. Toussaint remarked, "I told him to prune the tree, not to uproot it." By the time it ended, thousands were dead.

Toussaint knew that the French wanted to depose him, possibly using neighboring Santo Domingo as a staging area. Spain had ceded the colony to France when it withdrew its forces in 1795. Toussaint decided to invade and capture it himself, but in the name of

France, in 1801. His men encountered little resistance as they made their way across the island to the city of Santo Domingo. There Toussaint hoisted the flag of France and declared the colony annexed to Saint-Domingue. Then he declared an end to slavery in that part of the island. It was a special moment: Hispaniola, the first place in the New World to have African slaves, now saw the end of slavery.

Toussaint's audacious act was the last straw for Napoleon. He had long wanted to rid himself of "this gilded African." He also wanted to retake the island and use it as a staging area to colonize the Louisiana Territory. To achieve this goal, Napoleon dispatched sixty-seven ships with 21,000 of his best soldiers. On seeing the arriving fleet, Toussaint cried, "We are doomed! All France has come." As the French troops disembarked at the different coastal ports, they discovered that the towns were in ashes. Toussaint had given orders to burn everything, to pollute the wells with dead horses, to leave nothing that could be used. It was a costly war in which all of the work of reconstruction was again lost.

As the battles went on, the army of blacks was increasingly overwhelmed. Napoleon had given instructions to General Charles Leclerc, his brother-in-law and commander of the French forces, to bribe Toussaint's officers by offering to continue their positions in the French Army, as French officers, if they surrendered. Soon Henri Christophe, without supplies and his men exhausted, gave up the fight. Ten days later Toussaint, seeing the destruction of his dreams and wishing to stop additional massacres, agreed to surrender. He returned to his plantation home at Ennery, but on June 7, 1802, a French general arrested him. With his wife and children, Toussaint was placed aboard a ship bound for France. Once there he was conducted to Fort de Joux, an old Roman fortress high in the French Alps. He entered his cell on August 24, 1802, and was never allowed to leave. Stripped of his rank and dignity, he was rationed the secondhand clothes of a private. Throughout the cold winter when the temperature

Henri Christophe, a rebel general under Louverture.

dropped to twenty degrees below zero, he wrote letters to Napoleon protesting his unjust treatment, but his letters were never answered. As a last insult, Napoleon ordered that pen and paper be taken away. On April 7, 1803, an attendant at the prison found him dead.

Back in Saint-Domingue, just as Toussaint had said, the roots of the tree of liberty were springing up. Although Christophe, Dessalines, Pétion, and other generals were now in the service of their former enemies, new leaders were taking up the cause. Uprisings were occurring across the island. The French responded with a wave of killings. General Leclerc said openly, and in a letter to Napoleon, that in order to restore order in the colony every black and mulatto adult would have to be killed and new slaves brought in from Africa. The process of extermination began under Leclerc and, after his death from yellow fever, was continued by his successor, General Rochambeau, with even greater zeal and horror. Vicious bloodhounds, brought in from Cuba, were used to rip away the flesh of their victims. Blacks were roped together on rafts, taken out to sea, and drowned. Many were shot or hanged. It was for all purposes a festival of death.

But the resistance persisted. Soon Dessalines, Christophe, and the mulatto general Alexandre Pétion, defected to the new rebels. Black and mulatto resistance grew stronger while the morale of the

Alexandre Pétion, a general and president of Haiti, 1807–1818.

French army weakened. Like the British before them, French soldiers were ravaged by tropical diseases. Before it was over, at least 12,000 would die from yellow fever and malaria. The situation was made worse in July 1803, when England, again having declared war on France, blockaded French ships. Under attack from the high seas and from the high mountains, Rochambeau chose to surrender to the British in November 1803. With the departure of his troops, France saw the end of her colony.

On December 31, 1803, Jean-Jacques Dessalines, surrounded by twenty black and mulatto companions, declared the independence of the republic of Haiti. Toussaint Louverture did not live to see the

THE LIFE

OF

TOUSSAINT L'OUVERTURE,

The Negro Patriot of Hayti.

BY THE REV. JOHN R. BEARD, D.D.

MEMBER OF THE HISTORICO-THEOLOGICAL SOCIETY OF LEIPSIC, ETC

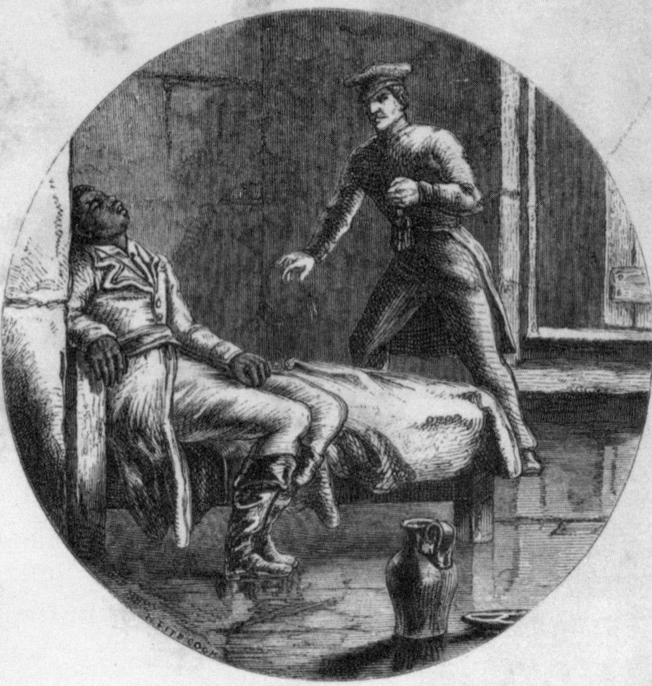

TOUSSAINT FOUND DEAD BY HIS GAOLER.

With numerous Engravings.

Toussaint L'Ouverture was found dead in his prison cell in France on April 7, 1803.

glorious event, but it was he, more than anyone else, who made it possible. Although British and American officials attempted to prevent information about Toussaint from reaching their slaves, throughout the Caribbean and in the United States blacks heard the story of Toussaint, "First of the Blacks," and so gained courage for their own struggles against slavery and oppression.

4

GABRIEL PROSSER

As word of Toussaint Louverture's triumphs and rise to power in the French colony spread north, slaves in the United States took heart and their spirits were uplifted. The struggle against slavery in Haiti was also a source of pride and inspiration to the oppressed class of free blacks.

Doubtlessly encouraged by news from the Caribbean, the free black community of Philadelphia, in a bold attempt to exercise the political rights of American citizens, sent a formal petition to the United States Congress in January 1800. Respectful and polite in tone, the document sought the gradual abolition of slavery. The request proved to be a futile effort. Harrison Gray Otis, a powerful congressman from Massachusetts, refused to let the petition come up for consideration. To acknowledge a petition from black people would, he reasoned, "teach [African Americans] the art of assembling together, debating and the like, and would soon extend from one end of the Union to the other." The House of Representatives voted 85 to 1 to offer "no encouragement or countenance to such message from people of color."

Meanwhile, in Henrico County, just outside Richmond, Virginia, three slave brothers were also moved to action by the Haitian revolutionaries.

Solomon, Martin, and Gabriel were owned by Thomas Prosser, a tavern keeper. In 1800, Gabriel, the youngest, was twenty-four. Taller than his two brothers, he stood six feet two inches, with striking African features. Armed with literacy and a gift for speaking, he became a convincing leader and organizer.

Gabriel and his brother Martin, who was a preacher, read whatever they could get their hands on about Haiti, often reading out loud to groups of slaves who cheered and applauded as the scenes unfolded. Every now and then, Gabriel would pause and plant seeds of rebellion. First, he'd praise Toussaint for being a great leader. Then Gabriel would remind his listeners that Toussaint had been a slave, just like them. His army had been fellow slaves, just like them. If Toussaint could do it, then why not they? If it could happen in Haiti, then why not in Virginia? It started the slaves thinking, and that's just what Gabriel wanted.

Gabriel and Martin also used Bible stories and truths to present daring ideas. At funerals and other religious meetings, Gabriel's muted voice could be heard teaching how Moses led the people of Israel out of bondage in Egypt. No doubt they sang songs about it:

Go down, Moses,
Way down in Egypt land.
Tell ol' Pharaoh
To let my people go.

Every slave knew Gabriel wasn't really talking about Pharaoh, but about the condition of slaves right there in Virginia. And to the slaves who longed to be free, Gabriel's voice was like the trumpet of the archangel Gabriel, God's messenger.

Gabriel knew that it would take a powerful message to convince slaves to go against all they had been taught to believe about themselves and their masters. Some thought their masters held magical powers and could hear their thoughts. Others believed that their plantation was surrounded by a wide ocean. Using truth and common sense as his tools, Gabriel slowly chipped away at these fears and superstitions.

In time, Gabriel began revealing his plan for a revolt. He shared it first with his brothers, then with close friends and associates. He hoped that by a surprise attack on Richmond, he could capture arms, burn warehouses, and perhaps take the governor, James Monroe, hostage. Beyond that, it isn't clear what Gabriel had in mind to do. As a rule rebels never revealed too much at one time or to too many people because of the ever-present fear of informers.

There is some speculation of foreign agents, probably French, who promised substantial assistance, based on Gabriel's ability to muster slave support. There is also evidence that he contacted the Catawba Indians. Virginia authorities later came to suspect that he was even helped by slaves who had been brought from Haiti to Virginia. Here, Gabriel's naiveté is revealed. He either didn't know or couldn't comprehend the extent to which the power of the federal government could and would be used to put down an insurrection, regardless of who supported it.

Gabriel asked his brother Solomon to make weapons, and he assigned fellow slaves Jack Bowler and

Slaves who were newly brought from Africa kept their music and dance traditions.

Ben Woolfolk to be recruiters. Bowler suggested that Gabriel incorporate some of the outlanders, a term referring to slaves who were newly arrived from Africa and who were customarily kept at some distance from the plantation houses. Because they knew only the customs and traditions of their African homelands, their ways seemed strange to American-born slaves. As a devout Christian, Gabriel disapproved of the religious practices of the outlanders, and, for this reason, he excluded them.

After months of planning, the time of the revolt was set for midnight, August 30, 1800. The night before, Gabriel gave his inner circle of leaders their final orders. They were to take Richmond and kill any man, woman, or child who tried to stop them. Spared from this massacre would be the French who had taught them "liberty, equality, fraternity"; the Quakers and Methodists who had "shone them mercy and were believers in justice"; and poor whites whose conditions were not much better than the slaves'. He planned to carry a silk flag with the words "Death or Liberty," based on the motto of Haitian revolutionaries. Virginians would also recognize the statement, for it was Patrick Henry who had said, "Give me liberty or give me death," just a few decades earlier. Gabriel ended by giving the command: "Arise! Arise! Shake off your chains!"

At the appointed time, Gabriel was said to have

had over a thousand recruits ready to answer his call to arms; others gave a lower number. There is much speculation about what might have happened if Gabriel's plan had been put into action. But we'll never know for sure, because in the end both man and nature betrayed him.

At noon on the 30th it began to rain — a steady downpour that lasted well into the night. The rivers and creeks flooded and blocked all roads. Gabriel called off the revolt, but on such short notice it was impossible to get the message out to all those involved. His people were confused and frightened. At the end of the storm, it was too late to reorganize because two slaves had divulged the plot.

Pharoah and Tom, slaves at Meadow Farm, told their master, Mosby Sheppard, about the planned insurrection. Sheppard informed Governor Monroe.

The conspirators were hurriedly rounded up, but Gabriel managed to escape with the help of the captain of a coastal schooner, the *Mary*. A slave onboard recognized the rebel and turned him in. Gabriel was captured in Norfolk in September 1800. The captain claimed he didn't know Gabriel was a fugitive, but there is enough evidence to suggest that he did. Either way, Gabriel remained silent, never offering one iota of information about the details of his planned revolt.

When he was returned to Richmond, Gabriel

learned that his brothers and others had been captured. The only brother to break the silence was Solomon, whose confession is a matter of record:

> *Communications made to the subscribers by Solomon, the property of Thomas Prosser, of Henrico, now under sentence of death for plotting an insurrection.*
>
> *My brother Gabriel was the person who influenced me to join him and others in order that (as he said) we might conquer the white people and possess ourselves of their property. I enquired how we were to effect it. He said by falling upon them (the whites) in the dead of night, at which time they would be unguarded and unsuspicious. I then inquired who was at the head of the plan. He said Jack, alias Jack Bowler. I asked him if Jack Bowler knew anything about carrying on war. He replied he did not. I then inquired who he was going to employ. He said a man from Caroline who was at the siege of Yorktown, and who was to meet him (Gabriel) at the Brook and to proceed on to Richmond, take and then fortify it. He applied to me to make scythe-swords, which I did to the number of twelve. Every Sunday he came to Richmond to provide ammunition and to find where the military stores were deposited.*

Gabriel informed me, in case of success, that they intended to subdue the whole of the country where slavery was permitted, but no further.

The first places Gabriel intended to attack in Richmond were the Capitol, the Magazine, the Penitentiary, the Governor's house and his person. The inhabitants were to be massacred, save those who begged for quarter and agreed

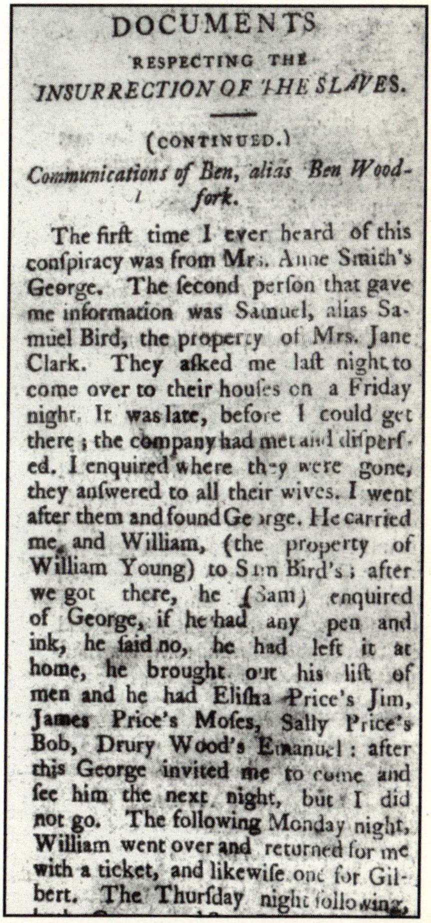

DOCUMENTS

RESPECTING THE

INSURRECTION OF THE SLAVES.

(CONTINUED.)

Communications of Ben, alias Ben Woodfork.

The firſt time I ever heard of this conſpiracy was from Mrs. Anne Smith's George. The ſecond perſon that gave me information was Samuel, alias Samuel Bird, the property of Mrs. Jane Clark. They aſked me laſt night to come over to their houſes on a Friday night. It was late, before I could get there; the company had met and diſperſed. I enquired where they were gone, they anſwered to all their wives. I went after them and found George. He carried me, and William, (the property of William Young) to Sam Bird's; after we got there, he (Sam) enquired of George, if he had any pen and ink, he ſaid no, he had left it at home, he brought out his liſt of men and he had Eliſha Price's Jim, James Price's Moſes, Sally Price's Bob, Drury Wood's Emanuel: after this George invited me to come and ſee him the next night, but I did not go. The following Monday night, William went over and returned for me with a ticket, and likewiſe one for Gilbert. The Thurſday night following,

A newspaper report on April 9, 1803, of a slave insurrection.

to serve as soldiers with them. The reason why the insurrection was to be made at this particular time was, the discharge of the number of soldiers one or two months ago, which induced Gabriel to believe the plan would be more easily executed.

Given under our hand this 15th day of September 1800.

Gervas Storrs
Joseph Selden

It is difficult to determine how much of this testimony is true. Very often confessions were written based on what the authorities believed happened. The prisoner was forced to sign the statement which was then submitted as evidence.

When Governor James Monroe, later president of the United States, left from visiting Gabriel, he wrote: "[Gabriel] seems to have made up his mind to die . . . and to have resolved to say but little on the subject of the conspiracy." He was hanged on October 7, 1800. At another time, place, and under different circumstances, Gabriel might have been a national hero. Instead he became the martyr of an oppressed people who heard in his voice the trumpet of freedom.

By all testimony given at the trial against Gabriel, one thing is clear. He was definitely influenced by Toussaint Louverture. But Gabriel wasn't the only one. In 1801 a slave named Arthur was captured after his attempted revolt was again halted by betrayal. He died on the gallows quoting Toussaint.

Then, in 1811, Charles Deslondes, a free black who had been in Haiti, organized close to five hundred slaves. Armed with scythes, sticks, and stones, they burned plantations and fields as they marched toward New Orleans. When confronted by the militia, they

James Monroe, who would later become president, visited Prosser before he was hung.

held them off for eleven days before they were subdued. It was the largest slave uprising on record in the country.

After Deslondes's defeat, there were no trials. He and his men were killed, beheaded, and their heads impaled on poles along the road for sixty miles.

By 1820, the internal struggle over the question of slavery had intensified. In an effort to appease both sides, Congress approved a compromise, stating slavery would not be permitted north and west of the 36° 30′ parallel line — known as the Mason-Dixon line. Missouri entered the Union as a slave state and Maine entered as a free state. Thomas Jefferson said the compromise was "like a fire bell ringing in the night." John Quincy Adams wrote in his diary that it was "morally and politically vicious."

Denmark Vesey, a free black man living in Charleston, South Carolina, was one of those who closely followed the Missouri debate. He became convinced that there was no peaceful way to end slavery.

5

DENMARK VESEY

Toussaint Louverture's rebellion and the biblical account of Moses and the delivery of the Hebrews from slavery in ancient Egypt inspired the same confidence in Denmark Vesey just as they had in Gabriel.

Gabriel was motivated by the general idea of a successful slave revolt. However, Denmark Vesey was more interested in Toussaint's leadership abilities. Vesey, who could read and write and speak several langauges, studied Toussaint's strategies and tactics — including his strengths and weaknesses — with the hope that what he learned might help him become a strong leader.

Like Gabriel, Vesey was a literate man, uncommonly talented and sophisticated. Just to look at him nobody would suspect that he was at the center of a slave uprising.

Born either in Africa or the Caribbean between 1767 and 1770, Vesey was owned by a slave trader, Captain Joseph Vesey. For well over 14 years, he traveled to many countries, including Haiti, where he lived for three months. In 1800, the year of Ga-

Denmark Vesey's home in Charleston, South Carolina.

briel's revolt, Vesey, at age thirty, bought his freedom with money he'd won in a lottery. He settled in Charleston, South Carolina, on Bull Street where he operated a successful carpentry shop. Being an industrious man and an able carpenter, he had by 1817 amassed several thousand dollars, which made him a wealthy man by the standards of that day. Those who knew him best said he stayed in Charleston only because his wife and children were still held in slavery.

South Carolina (and other slave states) had passed a law stating that black children were born "under the condition of their mother." No matter how much money Vesey had, his children were still legally slaves because his wife was a slave. When he tried to buy his family's freedom, their master refused to sell it.

Vesey was a proud figure of a man, good-looking, tall and straight as an arrow. In spite of the prevailing attitudes about black inferiority, Vesey taught his children differently. Though he was courteous and considerate, he refused to bow to whites. Vesey loved Bible stories and enjoyed telling them to his children when they were allowed to visit. He also read to slaves who often gathered at his home. Then, after reading, he would apply the theme of the story to everyday life. "You are as good as any man," he told them.

"We are slaves," they would reply.

"And for saying so, you deserve to be enslaved," he'd fire back. "You will remain slaves as long as you believe you are!"

He lived what he talked. A devout member of the Methodist Church, Vesey could be seen walking to services on Sunday mornings, with his head held high, and his prayer book in hand. The dignity of his appearance served as an affront to those who preached the inferiority of blacks. Such overt pride, however, caught the attention of local authorities, always on the lookout for threats to the status quo.

It was the religious commitment of Vesey and others — and white fears about large assemblies of blacks in a church uncontrolled by whites — that ultimately led to his decision to attempt an insurrection.

The story began in Charleston where black Methodists outnumbered the white membership ten to one. Blacks held their own quarterly conferences and managed their own collections. Intent on maintaining both unity and segregation, white Methodist leaders disapproved of such displays of independence. In 1815 the church convention revoked many of the rights the black congregations had exercised. Angered by the decision, Morris Brown and other free blacks set out for Philadelphia to confer with Richard Allen who, with his companions (called Allenites), was attempting to establish a separate and independent denomination.

Richard Allen, a former slave, was in his own way very much a rebel. While a slave living in Delaware, he became actively involved in the Methodist society, a movement operating within the Church of England. In 1784, in the aftermath of the War of Independence, the society organized itself as the Methodist Episcopal Church. At the first meeting, Allen, then twenty-four, became a candidate for the ministry. In 1786 he bought his freedom and moved to Philadelphia where he affiliated himself with St. George's Methodist Episcopal Church. After a bitter dispute over segregated seating at the church, Allen and other black members bolted and formed their own congregation in 1787. In 1789 Allen became the first

African American to be ordained a minister in the Methodist Episcopal Church. After continuing frictions, including a lawsuit, the black congregation succeeded in gaining full independence in 1816 and became the African Methodist Episcopal (A.M.E.) Church. Allen was elected bishop.

Inspired by Allen, Morris Brown returned to Charleston and in 1817 started the Hampstead A.M.E. Church. Denmark Vesey became one of its founding members.

From the beginning the new church was viewed with suspicion. Local authorities constantly harassed members, asking questions, seeking reasons to close the church down. Meetings were interrupted and bro-

Richard Allen, the first bishop of the African Methodist Episcopal Church.

ken up. Spies were installed with instructions to report *everything,* no matter how small or insignificant it may have seemed. Still, over the next few years, six thousand blacks joined A.M.E. churches all over Charleston.

Then for no apparent good reason, in late 1821, Charleston authorities closed the Hampstead A.M.E. Church. Vesey began planning his rebellion. "We were deprived of our rights and privileges by the white people . . . our church was shut up so that we could not use it . . . it was high time for us to seek our rights . . . and we were fully able to conquer the whites if we were only unanimous and courageous as the Santo Domingo [Haitian] people were."

Vesey knew the danger of involving too many people in his plot. There was no way he could raise an army and expect it not to be exposed sooner or later, so he tried to plan well and move quickly, never revealing all of his plan to any one person — not even his most trusted allies.

His first strategy was to select lieutenants who could recruit large numbers of slaves, and who, when the revolt started, could lead their groups in the completion of their assigned operations.

Vesey chose Peter Poyas to be his second in command. Peter was a master ship carpenter who also had strong skills as an organizer. People trusted him and he was respected for his honesty and courage.

Vesey also entrusted Jack Pritchard, known as Gullah Jack, with the responsibility of reaching the outlanders. Vesey recognized that they would be more likely to follow Gullah Jack than him. Vesey was right.

Gullah Jack was an African-born conjurer who was said to practice traditional African magical arts. He used amulets and charms to win recruits and instill confidence in them, in the face of such daunting odds. The charms represented what every rebel needed . . . luck.

Slowly the conspiracy began to take shape. Peter Poyas warned Vesey not to involve house servants. Living in close proximity to the masters, they might, deliberately or by speaking too freely, divulge the plan. The core group was made up of skilled craftsmen, sailors, and free blacks. Each leader knew only a part of the plan, but none, except Vesey himself, knew all the details.

As Vesey busied himself handling other aspects of the insurrection, Poyas organized cells composed of a leader and a certain number of men. Recruits knew only the names of their leader and a vague outline of what they were going to be asked to do. In this way, if one person was caught, he would be unable to identify other participants or endanger the whole scheme. One group was to set fire to the governor's mills, along with some houses near the water. Fire bells would serve as signals for the others to start the assault. Striking from six points, bands of rebels

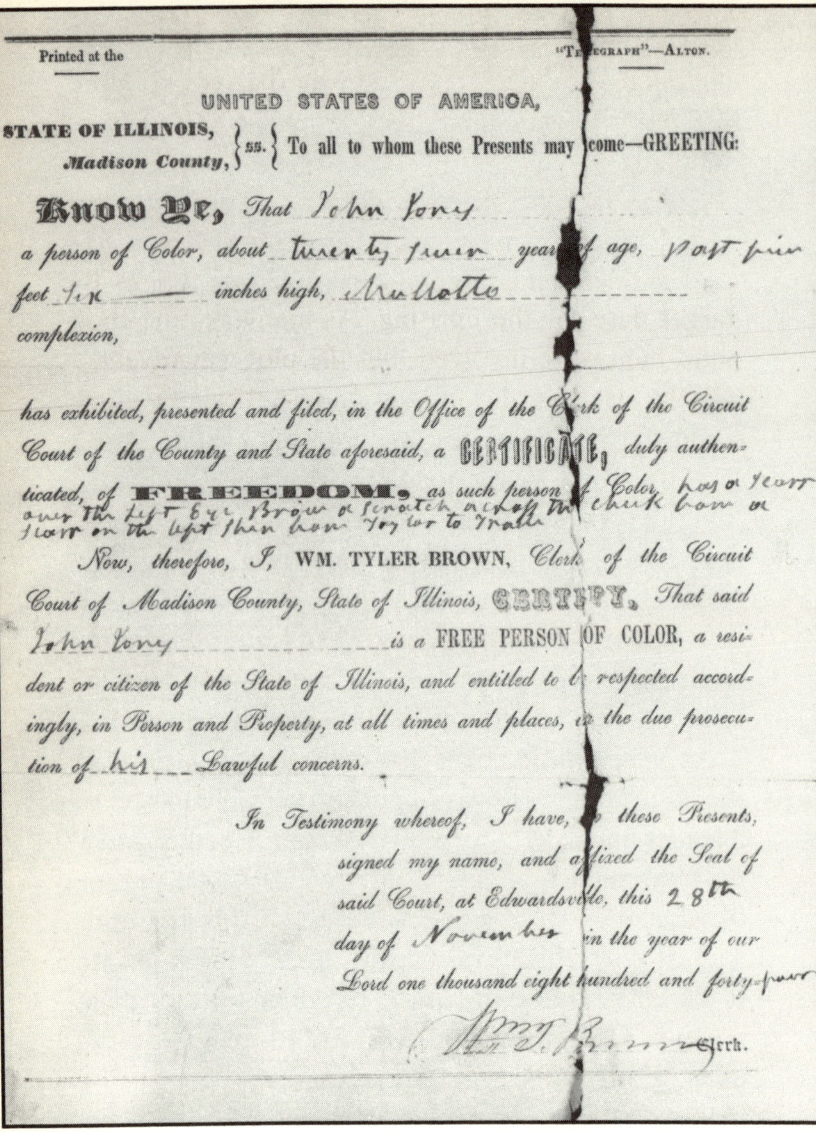

Printed at the "TELEGRAPH"—ALTON.

UNITED STATES OF AMERICA,

STATE OF ILLINOIS, Madison County, } ss. { To all to whom these Presents may come—GREETING:

Know Ye, That John Jones
a person of Color, about twenty four years of age, 5 foot five feet six inches high, Mullatto complexion,

has exhibited, presented and filed, in the Office of the Clerk of the Circuit Court of the County and State aforesaid, a **CERTIFICATE**, duly authenticated, of **FREEDOM**, as such person of Color, has a scarr over the left Eye Brow a scratch across the cheek bone a scarr on the left thum bone Taylor to trade

Now, therefore, I, WM. TYLER BROWN, Clerk of the Circuit Court of Madison County, State of Illinois, **CERTIFY**, That said John Jones is a FREE PERSON OF COLOR, a resident or citizen of the State of Illinois, and entitled to be respected accordingly, in Person and Property, at all times and places, in the due prosecution of his Lawful concerns.

In Testimony whereof, I have, to these Presents, signed my name, and affixed the Seal of said Court, at Edwardsville, this 28th day of November in the year of our Lord one thousand eight hundred and forty-four

Wm. T. Brown Clerk.

Freedom paper for John Jones, a "person of color."

would take possession of arsenals, guardhouses, powder magazines, and naval stores in Charleston. Meanwhile, other groups would move to capture ships in the harbor which would serve to carry the insurgents to freedom somewhere in the Caribbean (perhaps, Haiti).

The second Sunday in July 1822 was set as the target date for the uprising. As many as nine thousand men were involved, but the plot was revealed. On the last Saturday in May a house slave of Colonel John C. Prioleau learned about the revolt and reported it to Mrs. Prioleau. Within five days, Charleston authorities knew at least the bare bones of the plan, but they had no idea of the full picture. Vesey, working with his lieutenants to limit the damage, held meetings all through the night and tried to act normally during the day.

The investigation continued for several weeks. Then word came that Peter Poyas and another conspirator, Mingo Harth, were under suspicion. Normally, a slave who was under investigation — guilty or not — tried to run, thus admitting his guilt. But Poyas, in a bold move, went to the mayor's house and protested that his honor had been questioned. He demanded that he and his friend be questioned and cleared. The authorities were confused; guilty people didn't act so confidently. The two men were released.

Vesey continued with his plan, but the date was

moved up to Sunday, June 16. Fear had spread through the ranks and three of his primary leaders broke their vow of silence and implicated Vesey in exchange for immunity. These men knew enough to do damage.

When the authorities realized the extent of the conspiracy, they were horrified. Governor Thomas Bennett requested federal assistance. Secretary of War John C. Calhoun, who was from South Carolina, sent troops from St. Augustine to Charleston. Calhoun didn't notify President James Monroe, even though only the president had the constitutional authority to send federal troops into states.

Vesey and five of his lieutenants were captured on June 22, 1822. Later over 313 people were arrested. Vesey was tried by a jury of two judges and three white citizens formed "for the better ordering and governing of Negroes and other slaves in this state." Only one core leader confessed; the rest remained calm — almost detached from the proceedings. Showing no fear and expressing no anxiety, they sat in stony silence as former companions, hoping for clemency, testified against them.

In the end they were all sentenced to death. Peter Poyas, dignified to the end, asked only that he be allowed to see his family before being hanged.

Vesey was the most puzzling to the slaveholding community. He had been a free man, yet he was willing to risk his life to free slaves. All too often the white authorities had come in contact with blacks who earned their freedom by betraying others. Not Vesey.

The judge in sentencing him said: "It is difficult to imagine what infatuation could have prompted you to attempt an enterprise so wild and visionary. You were a free man; were comparatively wealthy; and enjoyed every comfort, compatible with your situation. You had therefore much to risk and little to gain. From your age and experience you ought to have known that success was impracticable."

Many blacks came to the trial and federal troops stood by to stop any rescue attempts. The conspirators were hanged on July 3, 1822. Vesey died never revealing one single detail of his plot. At age fifty-five he had, in the name of freedom, chosen to die a rebel against slavery.

On the gallows, Peter Poyas called out to the others: "Do not open your lips! Die silent, as you shall see me do."

Further investigations resulted in the hanging of thirty-five more blacks. Forty-two free blacks were forced to leave the city, among them Morris Brown. Brown fled to the North and, in 1828, succeeded Richard Allen as Bishop of the A.M.E. Church.

The South Carolina legislature reacted frantically in the aftermath of the Vesey plot by outlawing the A.M.E. Church and its ministers. Laws were passed to prevent the return of free blacks who had left the state. The most drastic move was the imprisonment of black seamen during the time that their vessels were in a South Carolina harbor. Even though the Black Seaman's Act was found illegal by a federal court, the practice continued.

Other slave states didn't respond to Vesey's conspiracy with additional laws, but the South was beginning to feel the pressure of another rebel group that was growing in number: the abolitionists.

6

REBEL ABOLITIONISTS

The movement to end slavery began the moment it started. According to historian Herbert Aptheker, "The abolitionists were revolutionists."

African Americans were the first and the most lasting abolitionists, said Aptheker.

> *Their conspiracies and insurrections, individual struggles, systematic flights, maroon communities, efforts to buy freedom, cultural solidarity, creation of anti-slavery organizations and publications — all preceded white involvement. . . . Without the initiative of the Afro-American people, without their illumination of the nature of slavery, without their persistent struggle to be free,*

the abolitionist movement would have been a very different one.

Quaker women were among the first to take a stand against slavery. They rebelled against their own community by starting schools for black children and writing about the evils of slavery under assumed male or generic names. At first these women were considered fanatics and troublemakers, and few people, especially Southerners, took them seriously. But, by 1800, white males, many of whom held positions of power, had joined ranks with black abolitionists and their women allies. By the 1840s the movement was a force to be reckoned with.

Scores of abolitionist movements sprang up, such as the African Abolition Freehold Society, the African Female Anti-Slavery Society, and others. The

A rally of the American Anti-Slavery Society in Syracuse, New York, in the 1840's.

most famous of the organizations was the American Anti-Slavery Society, whose members included William Lloyd Garrison, founder and editor of *The Liberator,* Wendell Phillips, Lucretia Mott, Lydia Maria Child, Maria Chapman, Sojourner Truth, Robert Purvis, James Forten, and Frederick Douglass, the famous orator and editor of *The North Star,* an anti-slavery journal.

As more and more people were convinced that slavery needed to be ended, the rolls of the anti-slavery organizations increased. The scope and purpose of these groups varied. Although they all shared the general belief that slavery should be abolished, they differed on how and when it should be accomplished.

Some abolitionists advocated the gradual emancipation of slaves by a set date in the future, much the way Northern states had done. There were those who felt that slavery could and should be ended by a constitutional amendment. Others believed that boycotting the South would provide the economic pressure on slaveholders to force them to abandon their "peculiar institution."

Another group generated widespread support and controversy by calling for the resettlement of free blacks in West Africa. Although this Back to Africa movement seemed to offer a concern for the welfare of free blacks, it did nothing to put a stop to slavery itself. It was small wonder, then, that when the American Colonization Society was founded in December,

1816, two distinguished Southern senators — John C. Calhoun of South Carolina and Henry Clay of Kentucky — were among its sponsors.

The idea of returning to an African homeland appealed to many blacks. Captain Paul Cuffee, a sea captain, transported a group of fellow blacks to Sierra Leone in his own ship as early as 1815.

Cuffee's solution was not widely shared. Most blacks believed that a mass exodus of free blacks would leave the slaves deprived of support, only further strengthening the chains that held them in bondage. To protest the colonization efforts, a large group of free African Americans met in Philadelphia in Jan-

A newspaper article in 1815 about Captain Paul Cuffee's intended voyage to Africa.

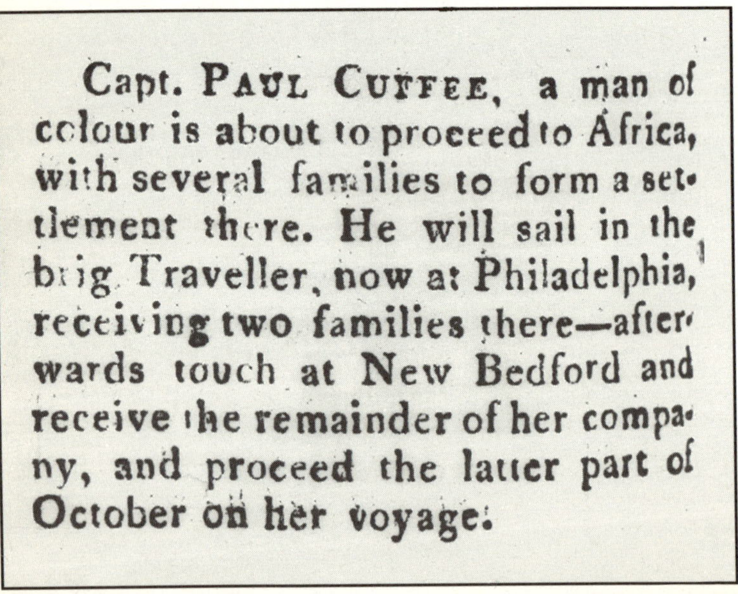

Capt. PAUL CUFFEE, a man of colour is about to proceed to Africa, with several families to form a settlement there. He will sail in the brig Traveller, now at Philadelphia, receiving two families there—afterwards touch at New Bedford and receive the remainder of her company, and proceed the latter part of October on her voyage.

uary 1817. Among the resolutions passed was the following:

> *Whereas our ancestors (not of choice) were the first successful cultivators of the wilds of America, we their descendants feel ourselves entitled to participate in the blessings of her luxuriant soil, which their blood and sweat manured; and that any measure or system of measures, having a tendency to banish us from her bosom, would not only be cruel, but in direct violation of those principles, which have been the boast of this republic . . .*

By 1830, the Back to Africa movement was revitalized. Once again, blacks and leading abolitionists rejected the idea because it would weaken the struggle against slavery itself.

As the debate intensified, a militant faction within the abolitionist movement emerged. Free men of color in New York, Boston, and Philadelphia became more daring in their encouragement of resistance. From pulpits and podiums they delivered their fiery messages that slavery had to be abolished immediately. If the slaveholders refused, then they called for armed resistance. They began publishing these ideas in journals and pamphlets, some of which were slipped into the South, where anxious black readers learned that they were not forsaken.

One such rebel abolitionist was David Walker who was born free on September 28, 1785, in Wilmington, North Carolina. Two horrible encounters with slavery had sealed his hatred of the institution and inspired his life-long dedication to its end. Walker saw (although some sources suggest that he was told about) a son forced to strip his mother naked and beat her until she died. And in another case, he saw an overseer beat a pregnant woman. Walker was convinced that he could not live among people who could exercise such absolute authority over his life. "If I remain in this bloody land," he said, "I will not live long." In 1826, Walker moved to Boston and opened a secondhand clothing store on Brattle Street.

Although he was forty-one years old he had never married, not from lack of looks or personal charm. Walker was a tall, slender man with strong, dark features. He was not quick to smile, but it was pleasant when he did.

Right away Walker joined the abolitionists and became a lecturer for the Massachusetts General Colored Association. He was consumed by ideas and spent hours each day poring over books of philosophy, logic, law, and the Bible.

From his studies, Walker concluded that slavery was a universal evil that mocked God's basic commandments. It had to be destroyed everywhere it existed. To him the abolition of slavery became a holy crusade: "I believe God has something in reserve

John B. Russwurm, who cofounded Freedom's Journal, *the first black newspaper in New York City.*

for us, which when he shall have poured out upon us, will repay for all our suffering and misery."

The Bible and the great philosophers provided him with all the support he needed for his beliefs. "The souls of those who call themselves Christians," he said, "and claim to know God's teachings, yet deliberately keep human beings in bondage, will stand in God's judgment. . . . Can the Americans escape God Almighty? If they do, can he be to us a God of justice?" The answer was clear to him. "God is just and I know it — for he has convinced me to my satisfaction — I cannot doubt him."

In 1827, the year after his arrival in Boston, Walker met John B. Russwurm. Russwurm and Samuel Cornish published the first black newspaper in New York City, titled *Freedom's Journal.* At first, Walker was a welcome contributor. But the tone of his articles was considered too radical. He wrote that for slaves to "rise up in revolt" was an "act of self-defense." Russwurm and Cornish tried to refocus the paper "to make an impact through sound advocacy of the black cause." For Walker, advocacy was not enough; blacks needed to *do* something.

True to his word, Walker was a man of action. He worked in his store, and made his house a safe heaven for runaways who needed his help. He continued to read and write, and speak at meetings.

Walker's life was dedicated to the end of slavery, but he was also deeply concerned about racism. In 1829 over two million blacks lived in bondage; but in the Northern cities, free African Americans faced racism and discrimination on a daily basis. It was difficult for free blacks to get an education, find a good job or decent housing.

When the Back to Africa debate resurfaced, John B. Russwurm argued that it was a "waste of words to talk of ever enjoying citizenship in this country." At an address before the Massachusetts General Colored Association, Walker rejected the idea. Instead he called for blacks to organize, saying, "Ought we not to form ourselves into a general body to protect, aid, and assist each other to the utmost of our power?"

To put forward his ideas, Walker published *Walker's Appeal, in Four Articles: Together with a Preamble, to the Coloured Citizens of the World, but in particular and very expressly, to those of the United States of America, September 28, 1829.* For practical purposes it was referred to simply as *Walker's Appeal.*

The title page of Walker's Appeal, *published in 1829.*

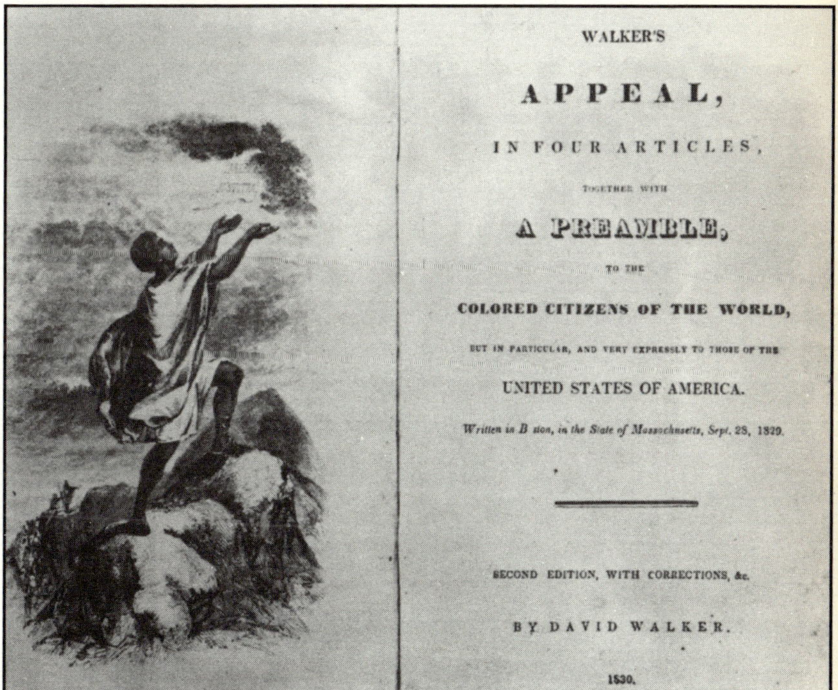

WALKER'S

APPEAL,

IN FOUR ARTICLES,

TOGETHER WITH

A PREAMBLE,

TO THE

COLORED CITIZENS OF THE WORLD,

BUT IN PARTICULAR, AND VERY EXPRESSLY TO THOSE OF THE

UNITED STATES OF AMERICA.

Written in Boston, in the State of Massachusetts, Sept. 28, 1829.

SECOND EDITION, WITH CORRECTIONS, &c.

BY DAVID WALKER.

1830.

The themes of the *Appeal* can be summarized:

(1) God's judgment was unavoidable unless slavery was ended unconditionally.
(2) Blacks needed to recognize that by not fighting for their freedom they were accepting slavery, allowing it to continue.
(3) People of color should take the lead in ending slavery and racism. To do so, they needed to become more unified in their efforts.
(4) Blacks needed to become more educated — never stop learning.
(5) All people of color throughout the world should be willing to fight and die for freedom and justice.

At the end Walker wrote: "Kill or be killed." But he warned, "If you commence, make sure work of it — do not trifle, for they will not trifle with you. . . ."

Such words were terrifying to Southerners. The governors of Virginia, Georgia, and North Carolina called special sessions of their legislatures to discuss Walker's words, and a number of Southern mayors asked Boston's mayor to lock Walker up and burn his book. The mayor didn't do it, but Walker was criticized by Northerners as well — some of them blacks who felt his language was too strong and devisive. Some felt he might scare off potential anti-slavery supporters. But Walker would not back down. "I will stand my ground. Somebody must die in this cause." Walker believed he was going to be assassinated and even wrote he was a "marked man."

It seems he was right in being fearful. On the morning of June 28, 1830, David Walker suddenly became ill and fell dead in the doorway of his shop. Most people believed the fearless crusader had been poisoned.

Walker's death was distressing to the growing number of militant black abolitionists because he had been the most eloquent spokesman for their position. But, in New York, a young pastor was gaining a reputation for being a radical in the tradition of Walker.

Henry Highland Garnet, unlike Walker, had been born a slave. When Henry was a toddler, his father, George, had learned that the family was going to be split up and sold. In a daring scheme, his father obtained written passes to attend a funeral and escaped with his family to New York City in 1825. Henry signed on as a cabin boy on a ship and went to sea. Unfortunately while he was away, a relative of their old slave master tracked the family to New York. George Garnet leaped from a window and escaped. Neighbors intervened and the family was spirited away to safe houses on Long Island.

Henry returned to an empty house and learned from a neighbor what had happened. Years later,

Henry Highland Garnet, who was inspired by David Walker.

Garnet said that incident was what made him become a rebel against slavery. In time the Garnet family was reunited.

Henry was enrolled in the New York African Free School, established by the New York Manumission Society in 1787. Those who knew him said that Henry Garnet was the brightest of the bright. He had uncommon abilities in writing and speaking. The boy showed such promise as a scholar that Reverend Theodore S. Wright, a prominent black Presbyterian minister, became his mentor. It was through Wright that young Garnet became interested in the ministry and the abolitionist movement.

After graduation from the Free School in 1835, Garnet and two other classmates were invited to attend Noyes Academy. The trip to Canaan, New Hampshire, was a long and difficult journey because the boys had to get there on foot. They were not welcomed in small towns, and there were no places to get food or shelter along the way, and Garnet was bothered by pain in his leg. But, he forced himself to keep up with the others. They were young and energetic and made do with what was provided: They ate fruits and berries, drank from springs, and slept under the stars.

They reached Canaan on the Fourth of July, only to find that a group of farmers had decided to close the school. They didn't want blacks living among them. So, they hitched ninety oxen and dragged the building off its foundation and pulled it to a nearby swamp.

The boys, fourteen in all, hid in their boardinghouse. Some of them were paralyzed by fear. Nineteen-year-old Henry became a leader. He knew the farmers would come for them next, and if they were going to make it out alive, they had to have a plan.

They found an old musket in the attic of the house, but there was no ammunition. One of the boys knew how to mold musket balls. As night fell, they waited in the darkness. Voices called out to the boys, making threats. Then out of the darkness, a lone rider sped past and shot at the house. A bullet lay on the floor, as other bullets zinged past them and lodged in the wall. At that moment, Garnet rushed to the window and fired the old musket into the darkness. There was a long period of silence. The men, not really knowing how much firing power the boys had, left for the night. At daybreak, the boys quickly left town, but a mob shot a cannon at their departing wagon.

Years later, Garnet revealed that he was frightened but invigorated at the same time. "I was fighting back!" he said.

Determined more than ever to go to school, Henry attended Oneida Theological Institute in Whiteboro, New York. He studied there for three years under Beriah Green, an abolitionist who believed in the full emancipation of slaves without delay. Green recognized Garnet's brilliance and encouraged him to become more active.

Green often spoke at conferences and meetings. He began taking Garnet with him, and encouraging the young man to speak about his ideas. During the late 1830s, Garnet made quite a name for himself speaking on the circuit. Like Walker, he believed that oppressed people needed to take the lead in their own liberation.

At the seventh anniversary of the American Anti-Slavery Society, Green arranged for his former student to address the leading white abolitionists on the question of how slavery should end.

Garnet spoke passionately about the need for black people to take the lead in their own struggle. No matter how hard white abolitionists worked, he said, conditions would "remain the same, until we awaken a consciousness of a momentous responsibility. Others may be our allies," he added, "but the battle is ours."

By then, Garnet was an ordained minister in the Presbyterian Church. He was pastoring in a racially mixed church in Troy, New York. Garnet was not convinced then that the deliverance of his people had to be through violent action. "No," he said in 1842, "the time for a last stern struggle has not yet come. The finger of the Almighty will hold back the trigger, and his all powerful arm will sheathe the sword till the oppressor's cup is full." But, within a year, Garnet was advocating slave uprisings and open revolts. In 1843 he said, "Let your motto be resistance! Resistance! Resistance!"

Some historians believe he might have read (or reread) *Walker's Appeal* with a different eye. He had gone to Boston and visited Walker's home and met his widow. He was deeply moved by Walker's selfless devotion to the liberation of his people. Garnet noticed little things that told him a lot about the man: For example, in his writing and notes, Walker never spoke of the slaves as "them" or "they." He always used "we." This impressed Garnet so much, he began using the inclusive "we," when referring to slaves.

In 1848, Garnet edited a version of *Walker's Appeal*. In it he added his own support to Walker's:

> *You had better all die — die immediately, than live slaves and entail your wretchedness upon your posterity. If you would be free in this generation, here is your only hope. . . . In the name of God, we ask, are you men? Where is the blood of your father? Has it all run out of your veins? Awake, awake! Millions of voices are calling you! Your dead fathers speak to you from their graves.*

His publication raised just as much criticism as Walker's first printing had, but it was received among the militants with enthusiasm. Garnet often said that if his leg hadn't been amputated in 1840 he would have gone South to organize a rebellion. He didn't have to go, however, for there was already another man who was planning a revolt in Southampton, Virginia.

7

NAT TURNER

Benjamin Turner owned a farm in Southampton County, Virginia, near the Dismal Swamp, where a group of runaways known as "the outlyers" lived. These runaways, unlike those maroons who tried to establish distant and hidden communities, were bandits who, under the cover of night, slipped back to the plantations to steal and terrorize both whites and blacks. Although they were outlaws the outlyers were free, and Nat Turner's father was probably one of them.

Nat Turner was born on October 2, 1800 — the year of Gabriel's conspiracy and Denmark Vesey's freedom. Nat's paternal grandmother, Old Bridget, helped raise him after his father ran away — probably to the Dismal Swamp. Nat's mother, Nancy, was from Africa, brought to Virginia in 1795 and purchased by Turner in 1799.

"They strengthened me," Turner said of his family. Old Bridget was wise and gave the boy her knowledge of roots and herbs for healing purposes. Nat's mother believed in the "old ways" from Africa. She believed in reading prophetic signs. She must have seen something at Nat's birth, because according to him, "She told me I was here for some great purpose."

In 1810, Turner's master died, and his son Samuel became his master. By 1822 Nat Turner had married Cherry, but was then sold to Thomas Moore for $400 and taken to his farm near Flat Swamp in the western part of the county. Giles Reese, a neighbor of Moore's, bought Cherry. When Moore died in 1828, twenty-eight-year-old Turner became the property of Moore's nine-year-old son, Putnam. (Some sources state Putnam was an infant.) The widow Sally Moore then married Joseph Travis who became master of the house in 1829. Thus, in 1831, Nat Turner — though legally still owned by the child Putnam — was under the authority of Joseph Travis.

How a slave was treated was dictated by the master's own beliefs and personality. If he was a cruel person by nature, he was cruel to his slaves as well. If he was prone to be kind and fair, he might deal with his slaves in the same manner. Against the advice of some masters, Benjamin and Samuel Turner had allowed their slaves to worship with the whites, but in a separate seating arrangement. As a child, Nat had attended church regularly and in the process he had learned to read and write. He also thought that he might like to become a preacher himself.

When Nat was in his early teens he began having dreams; before long his dreams were daylight visions. In one, as he described it: "White spirits and black

A charcoal sketch of Nat Turner after his arrest.

spirits were engaged in a battle and the sun was in darkness — the thunder rolled in the Heavens and blood flowed in streams — and I heard a voice saying, 'Such is your luck, such you are called to see, and let it come rough and smooth, you must surely bare [sic] it.' "

His ability to "see things" made Turner special among the slaves. They looked up to him, and sought his advice. With the knowledge his grandmother had taught him about healing roots and herbs, Turner became a well-respected root doctor. He was a fine preacher as well. He was a loner, never drank, smoked, or swore. In all ways he was even-tempered, calm, and helpful.

Sometimes Nat ran away to the woods where he would meditate and read. He always came back, so his master never worried much about where he was or how long he was gone. Contrary to what people said of him, he was not a maniac, full of rage and anger. He was a man with a purpose, and that purpose was freedom and he had a plan.

On Monday, August 22, 1831, Nat Turner and six fellow slaves began an insurrection that would rock the foundation upon which slavery was built.

After Turner was captured some months later, Thomas R. Gray, a lawyer, local horse breeder, and owner of Round Hill plantation, northeast of Jerusalem, interviewed Turner before and during his trial. Later Gray published *The Confessions of Nat Turner,* a pamphlet containing the story of Nat Turner's rebellion from his own point of view. Some say Gray was motivated by the prospect of making money, for he was in deep debt; others say he wanted to be a part of history, and still others felt he was genuinely interested in getting the story. For whatever reason Gray was inspired to write, *The Confessions of Nat Turner* give us a great deal of information about the man.

According to Turner, he had been divinely inspired to lead a rebellion. He said when he walked through the fields he saw blood in the leaves and he heard the wailing of voices in the winds; then he saw a sign in the heavens and "the seal was removed from my lips and I communicated the great work laid out for me to do. . . ." This is how the insurrection came about according to his confession.

Nat said since he was considered a preacher, he was allowed to attend funerals and worship services with his master's permission. Nat used this opportunity to recruit men to join him. At first he set July 4, 1831 as the day of attack, but he became ill — probably from anxiety. The time passed. Haunted by indecision and doubt, Turner delayed the attack again. Then on August 13 there was an eclipse of the sun. This was Turner's last sign. "The black spot had passed over the sun, so would the blacks pass over the earth."

He set August 22 as the day of revolt. (The date

HORRID MASSACRE IN VIRGINIA.

The Scenes which the above Plate is designed to represent, are---Figure 1. a Mother intreating for the lives of her children, ---2. Mr. Travis, cruelly murdered by his own Slaves.---3. Mr. Barrow, who bravely defended himself until his wife escaped ---4. A company of mounted Dragoons in pursuit of the Blacks.

Just Published, an Authentic and Interesting

NARRATIVE

OF THE

TRAGICAL SCENE

Which was witnessed in Southampton county (Virginia) on Monday the 22d of August last, when FIFTY FIVE of its inhabitants (mostly women and children) were inhumanly massacred by the Blacks!

Short and imperfect sketches of the horrid massacre above mentioned have appeared in the public Journals, but the public are now presented with every particular relative thereto, communicated by those who were eye witnesses of the bloody scene, and confirmed by the confessions of several of the Blacks while under sentence of death.

A more shocking instance of human butchery has seldom occurred in any country, and never before in this—the merciless wretches carried destruction to every white person they found in the houses, whether the hoary head, the lovely virgin, or the sleeping infant in the cradle! they spared none!—a widow (Mrs. Whitehead) and her 10 children were murdered in one house! among the slain on that fatal night, was an amiable young lady but 17 years of age, who the day following was to have been united in marriage to a young gentleman of North-Carolina, who had left home the evening preceding with the expectation of conveying there the succeeding day the object of his affections! but, alas! how sad was his disappointment! he was the third person who entered the house after the horrid massacre, to witness the mangled remains of her whom he was so shortly to espouse! The Blacks after having completed their work of death, attempted to evade the pursuit of those who had collected to oppose them, by secreting themselves in a neighboring swamp, to the borders of which they were pursued by a company of mounted dragoons. Of the fifty five slain nearly two thirds of the number were children, not exceeding twelve years of age! and it was truly a melancholly scene (as was observed to the writer by one who witnessed it) to behold on the day of their interment so great a number of coffins collected, surrounded by the weeping relatives!

While the friends of humanity however or wherever situated, cannot but sincerely and deeply lament the awful destruction of so many innocent lives, yet, the humane and philanthopic citizens of New-England, and of the middle States, cannot feel too thankful for the repose and peace of conscience which they enjoy, by wisely and humanely abolishing laws dooming a free born fellow being (without fault or crime) to perpetual bondage!---an example truly worthy of imitation by our brethren at the South.

The Narrative (which contains every important particular relating to the horrid massacre) is afforded for the trifling sum of 12 1-2 Cents.

☞ This paper left for perusal, and to be returned when called for.

An illustration from a pamphlet showing "scenes" from Nat Turner's rebellion, 1831.

was forty years to the day of the slave uprising that launched the Haitian Revolution.)

On the night of August 21, Turner, along with the slaves named Henry, Hark Travis, Nelson Williams, and Sam Francis, had a barbecue near Giles Reese's farm, Cabin Pond. At midnight, according to plan, they went to the Travis place, where they killed the family, took all the weapons, ammunition, and horses they could find and recruited several slaves to join them. Moving to the next house, they did the same thing. Their best ally was darkness and surprise, but even as they left the Travis farm, one of the slaves had slipped away and hurried to Nathaniel Francis's farm to warn him.

Turner and his rebel army marched toward the town of Jerusalem across Nottoway River; there he hoped to take the arms supply depot. Once the arms were captured, Turner planned to raid the larger plantations, recruit others, then escape into the Dismal Swamp where they could form a community and lead guerrilla warfare on the plantations.

Turner's numbers had increased to about fifty mounted and armed slaves. At James Parker's farm, less than three miles from Jerusalem, Turner's men met with armed opposition. In addition, a larger militia unit arrived within the half hour. Some of Turner's men scattered; several were wounded and captured. Several more were killed. Turner retreated in order to regroup.

The roads were blocked to Jerusalem now, so Turner's only hope was to hit the larger plantations where he might get fresh recruits. Doubling back to Bellfield in Greensville County, Turner, with about three dozen men at his side, exchanged volleys with the militia at Major Thomas Ridley's plantation. Once again Turner's men suffered hits, and some ran away. Needing to rest, Turner stopped to sleep. Many of his men used this opportunity to slip away.

When he woke, Turner had less than twenty men still ready to stand with him. In desperation, Turner moved against Dr. Simon Blunt's plantation, but he ran into stiff resistance there. Three of his men were killed. At about ten o'clock that morning, Turner sent his last four men to four different farms with the hopes that they could get recruits. They were to meet him at Cabin Pond with whoever would come back.

On Wednesday morning, when Turner arrived, there was no one there except a militia patrol. "On this I gave up hope for the present," he said. And he made his way to a nearby cave where he stayed for almost six weeks. While Turner was still at large, the South fell into a fit of fear and outrage.

Information about Nat Turner's rebellion has always been exaggerated by both blacks and whites. Whites in Petersburg, Virginia, reported that 500 slaves were marching their way. People were sure that Turner had an army waiting in the swamps ready to sweep down on the people and murder them in their sleep. The thought "of Ol' Nat coming in the night kept more than a few masters awake at night," a slave told a traveler at the time. Certainty that blacks could not have conceived or carried out such a revolt by themselves led the authorities to start looking for whites who might have helped. They were poised and ready to find a conspirator anywhere they could, and it led to some unfortunate situations, involving innocent people.

An Englishman was overheard to say that "the blacks like other men were entitled to their freedom." He was dragged from the stagecoach, stripped naked, beaten, then forced to walk into town. A poor white man was caught with a copy of William Lloyd Garrison's *The Liberator,* an abolitionist newspaper, in his home, and he was thrown into jail and charged with sedition.

Much of the worry was based on the unknown extent of the rebellion. One slaveholder reported that slaves were "out of control" over in Sampson County and Duplin County in North Carolina. In Alabama there were stories about Indian and black conspiracies.

Violations of "white womanhood" were a particular concern. The fact is women and children had been killed, but none were raped. According to historian Eugene Genovese, "In the slave revolts of the hemisphere as a whole, rape occurred rarely despite the blacks having had extreme provocation in the

Turner and his men hiding in the Dismal Swamp in Virginia.

constant violation of their own women by whites. . . . No one has found evidence of a single rape during the revolts in the United States."

Virginia Governor John Floyd's proclamation of September 17, 1831, offered $500 for the capture of Nat Turner. He was described as "the contriver and leader of the late insurrection." Stories had made Turner seem like a giant, but he was only about five feet six inches tall and, according to the wanted poster, he had several distinguishing scars, "one on his temple caused by a mule kick and one near his wrist produced by a blow."

Turner managed to elude an extensive manhunt until mid-October when two slaves were out hunting and their dog discovered his camp. The slaves recognized Turner and fled. Knowing he could not stay there, he found another hiding place underneath a fallen tree. He was pursued for several more weeks before a Benjamin Phipps captured Turner on Sunday, October 30, and took him to jail.

He pleaded not guilty, because he didn't "feel" guilty. After hearing evidence, Judge Jeremiah Cobb called for the prisoner to rise. Turner, a man with broad shoulders and thinning hair, pulled himself

Nat Turner was captured by Benjamin Phipps on October 30, 1831.

straight to receive his sentence. Death. He never flinched. Turner was hanged November 11, 1831.

Stories about Turner borderlined on the bizarre. The most controversial event surrounding Turner's death was about what happened to his body. Some whites swore that on the bottom of his foot there appeared a W. Those who saw it said it might have stood for War. A local doctor dissected his body to see if there was some biological reason for his rebellious nature. Parts of Turner's body were then passed out as souvenirs. In the quarters, slaves told the story that Turner said it would storm after his death, and it did rain, followed by a long dry spell. Folks started calling the drought "Nat's Revenge."

Naturally, contrasting tales grew up around his name and his deeds. Among whites he was feared and hated. Slaves honored him. Slaveholders forbade slaves to speak his name, and they were not allowed to name their children Nat or Turner. And to make it clear to all future Nat Turners, John Hampden Pleasants made the slaveholders' position quite clear. In the Richmond *Constitutional Whig,* Pleasants wrote: "Let the fact not be doubted by those whom it most concerns, that other such insurrection will be the signal for the extermination of the whole black population in the quarter of the state where it occurs."

It is interesting to note that Governor Floyd wrote in his diary, November 21, 1831, that he wished "to have a law passed gradually abolishing slavery in [his] state." More than a few people — in the South as well as the North — were leaning toward that solution, but slaveholders were the ruling class and they controlled the statehouses. Like Pharaoh whose heart was hardened when Moses told him to "Let my people go," slaveholders would not budge when it came to any form of abolition. If Virginia had begun a gradual emancipation process, other states might have followed, especially in Kentucky, Tennessee, and Maryland, and history might have been quite different.

8

CINQUE AND THE *AMISTAD*

The voyage across the Atlantic from Africa to the New World became known as the Middle Passage. It was filled with unimaginable horrors for the African captives who were put on board slave ships and transported thousands of miles from their home. Confused, and terrified of the unknown, the Africans often chose death by either refusing to eat or by leaping overboard. And whenever possible, they rose up against their captors and fought for their freedom.

According to one ship's log, dated 1693, "[We keep the slaves] shackled two and two while we lie in port and in sight of their own country, for 'tis then they attempt to make their escape and mutiny. We always keep sentinels upon the hatchways and have a chest full of small arms ready loaded. . . ."

Revolts and the threat of revolts on slave ships proved to be costly to investors. During the late seventeenth century, a group of Dutch traders established a set of rigidly enforced guidelines for the "safe transport of cargo [slaves]" and "the efficient management of a slave vessel on the high seas." For example, captives were stripped naked so nothing could be "concealed or fashioned into a weapon or instrument of self-destruction"; crew members were ordered to strap their "cutlasses to their wrists so they couldn't be snatched away easily"; and any captive found not eating was to be force-fed. By the mid-eighteenth century these guidelines were common practices onboard most European slavers. Yet no amount of precautions could stop Africans from resisting their captivity.

Given the slightest opportunity, Africans continued to overpower crews and force them to sail back to Africa or to a free port. Probably one of the most

"La Amistad," artist unknown, painted after 1839.

interesting mutinies was carried out on the Spanish slave ship, *Amistad.*

In the summer of 1839 — the same year the Seminoles and their black allies were forced from Tampa Bay, Florida, to the West — there were reports that a "long black schooner" manned by armed blacks was spotted off the cost of Montauk, New York. Lieutenant Richard Meade, on board the *U.S.S. Washington,* a revenue cutter, found the schooner on August 26, about a mile off Long Island, near Culloden Point.

Meade's commanding officer, Lieutenant Commander Thomas Gedney, ordered him to seize the ship, which he did. The Africans were captured and held along with two Spaniards named Pedro Montes and José Ruiz.

For Montes and Ruiz the story began in Havana, Cuba. The *Amistad,* loaded with fifty-three Africans, left for a South American slave market with intermediate stops at Caribbean ports along the way. On the third night out, the slaves rebelled. Led by the man known as Cinque (Seen-Kay), the captives killed the cook and the captain, Ramon Ferrer, but spared the life of the cabin boy, Antonio. Two crew members escaped in a lifeboat, and Montes and Ruiz were held as hostages.

Through the use of gestures, Cinque ordered Montes and Ruiz to sail the ship back to Africa. The Spaniards sailed toward the rising sun during the day,

Joseph Cinque, "who prefers death to slavery."

but at night they sailed northeast, hoping to come to a North American port.

Meade ordered the ship taken to Connecticut. Why Connecticut, when New York was closer? In New York slavery was not legal; in Connecticut slavery was still legal. Though fewer than twenty slaves actually lived in the state, slavery still had not been officially abolished by law in Connecticut.

Meade and Gedney hoped to legally claim the ship's cargo as salvage. In Connecticut that cargo might be judged to include the Africans, who were worth about $20,000. That's why Gedney sailed the *Amistad* into the harbor at New London, Connecticut, on August 27.

The Africans had no idea where they were or what was to happen to them next. Cinque frequently tried to make himself understood, but he couldn't make sense of the words that were being spoken around him. Cinque spoke to his countrymen in the Mende language, telling them to stay calm and brave. They would need to draw from their Mende heritage the strength and skill to carry them through the ordeals that lay ahead. When the Africans cheered in response, their captors became afraid and separated Cinque from the others.

Isolated and terribly lonely, Cinque later admitted that the words he had spoken to his comrades had failed to console his weary spirit. He still longed for his wife and beautiful children, and wondered if he'd ever see them again.

Cinque and the *Amistad* Africans were unaware at the time that they had friends in this strange land. Upon hearing about their plight, a number of abolitionists mobilized to help. Most Americans, even those who opposed slavery on a personal basis, believed it was alright for other people to own slaves. In 1839, out of a population of seventeen million people, there were less than 150,000 ablitionists. But as people learned more about slavery in lectures and meetings, attitudes were slowly changing. Abolitionists believed that the arrival of the *Amistad* would give them a chance to put the evils of slavery before the public in a bold and dramatic way.

United States District Court Judge Andrew Judson held a hearing on the *U.S.S. Washington,* August 29, 1839. He ordered that the adult Africans be tried in September before the United States Circuit Court in Hartford for the crimes of mutiny and murder. All the adults were ordered to New Haven where they were to be kept in jail awaiting trial.

According to one source, "A sideshow atmosphere" prevailed at the jail. People came from miles around and paid twelve-and-a-half cents to gawk at the prisoners.

In less than a week after Judson's decision, the *Amistad* Committee was organized by Reverend Joshua Leavitt, editor of the New York anti-slavery newspaper, *The Emancipator;* Reverend Simeon S. Jocelyn, a New Haven clergyman; and Lewis Tappan, a wealthy New York merchant and anti-slavery leader. Their first decision was to persuade Roger Sherman Baldwin, a New Haven lawyer, to head the defense team that would represent the Africans. Baldwin's grandfather, Roger Sherman, was a signer of the Declaration of Independence.

In order to prepare a defense, Baldwin needed to communicate with the Africans. Cinque was obviously the leader, and he seemed eager to cooperate, but how could they overcome the language barrier? With the help of scholars, Baldwin was able to iden-

A Mende village in Africa.

tify the language as Mende. Then they found an African who spoke some Mende, well enough to translate Cinque's story.

His story began not on a slave ship, but in the West African country of Sierra Leone, in the heart of the Mende culture. The Mende chose to live in Spartan conditions and rejected great displays of wealth. However, they appreciated art, music, and dance, and they were known for their craftsmanship.

The Mende had a democratic form of government in which both men and women participated. Individuals were granted rights similar to those in the United States Constitution's Bill of Rights. Since they had no monarchy, the Mende had a highly developed judicial system, complete with judges and juries. Trials were held publicly and decisions could be appealed.

Cinque was taught by his parents to value intelligence, strength, and persistence. He grew up honoring the virtues of silence and patience. At an appointed age, Cinque had passed through the *poro* system, which was at the center of Mende culture. Attaining membership in a secret society or *poro* was an important rite of passage into adulthood for Mende men and women. Cinque had spent several years preparing to be accepted into a *poro.* He and his peers were instructed in different subjects, including farming, ethics, and history, and they were expected to explore their own talents. Within the *poro,* leaders were elected; members pledged loyalty to the group. They provided for each other and each other's families in times of need and celebrated each other's triumphs and victories.

After this rite of passage, Cinque took his place within the larger community. Although he was in his early twenties, he was already a successful rice farmer, a prestigious occupation in Mende society; he was married and the father of several children. Then early in 1839, Cinque was captured while walking along the road. For a Mende man to be taken by treachery and deceit and not in battle was demeaning. He and forty-eight other young men, one boy, and three girls, most of them Mende, were captured by Spanish or Portuguese slave traders and taken to Lomboko off the western coast of Africa.

A Spaniard named Don Pedro Blanco operated an infamous center where annually he shipped thousands of Africans to North America. At Lomboko, Cinque was chained in the belly of a Portuguese slave ship, the *Tecora.* Perhaps as many as a third of the Africans died during the Middle Passage. Surrounded by stifling heat and darkness, Cinque called out words in Mende, trying to find out how many of his brothers were among the captives. He guessed fifty or more. Throughout the long and terrible voyage, the Mende men and women captives comforted each other with words of encouragement and hope.

Meanwhile up on deck, the captain was careful to dodge British sea patrols. By 1817, under Spanish law it was illegal to transport Africans to Cuba for sale as slaves. Slavers disregarded the law and bribed Cuban authorities who looked the other way.

The *Tecora* reached Havana in early summer. Ruiz and Montes purchased fifty-three of the Africans, including Cinque and several other Mende men and women, and herded them onto the *Amistad.* The ship's cook taunted Cinque with a cruel joke, gesturing that he and the others were going to be eaten when they arrived at their destination.

Below deck, the Mende chose Cinque to become their leader. On the third night out, Cinque and his

The death of Captain Ferrer of the Amistad, *July 1839.*

friend Grabeau pulled a nail from a loose board and used it to pick the locks on the iron collars fastened around their necks. They quickly freed the others.

Searching for whatever they could find, Cinque discovered a shipment of machetes — sugarcane knives with two foot long blades. Armed with these, the Africans rushed the sleeping crew, on July 1, 1839. There wasn't much of a fight. The captain was killed and the other crewmen fled on lifeboats.

After hearing Cinque's story, Baldwin knew he had a case. In September the *Amistad* Africans arrived in Hartford for trial on charges of mutiny and murder before the U.S. Circuit Court, presided over by Associate Justice Smith Thompson of the U.S. Supreme Court, and Judge Andrew Judson.

The trial opened at the state capitol. It was surprising to many, including the judge, how well Cinque understood the process of legal proceedings. None of them were intimidated by having to testify via the interpreter.

Justice Thompson ruled that the U.S. Circuit Court had no jurisdiction to try the Africans on the murder and mutiny charges, since the *Amistad* was a Spanish ship and the revolt had taken place in Spanish waters. The abolitionists were pleased with this verdict, but the battle had just begun.

What about the ship and its cargo? The Spaniards had a claim and so did Gedney and Meade. The judges referred the problem of untangling "the conficting claims on the ship and its cargo, particularly determining whether or not the Africans should be considered part of that cargo," to the U.S. District Court. The case went back to Judge Judson. The issue this time was: Were the *Amistad* Africans property, or were they people with rights? Abolitionists were not too hopeful about the outcome.

Judge Judson called the U.S. District Court into session immediately, then set a November trial date to allow time for examination of the claims. Baldwin asked that the Africans be released on bail. Judge Judson agreed, providing their bail covered the price they would bring in the Cuban slave market. The abolitionists refused to accept the terms, because to do so would be admitting the men were property, not human beings. Although they remained in custody, the African men were allowed to live in a house in New Haven and the women were housed in private homes.

Baldwin sought the help of Yale professor Josiah Willard Gibbs to help him more fully bridge the language gap between his clients and himself. Gibbs learned how to count in Mende; then he walked along New York City docks repeating the words aloud in the hope that someone would recognize them. James Covey heard the language of his childhood and approached Gibbs, hoping to converse more with him.

Covey was born a Mende, but as a young boy he had been captured and put on a ship bound for North America. However, the British patrol had intercepted the ship and rescued the captives. Covey had learned to speak, read, and write English at a missionary school in Sierra Leone, then signed on as a sailor on a British ship that was in port at the time he met Professor Gibbs. Covey returned to Hartford with Gibbs, and right away he proved to be invaluable. His translations were more accurate and more detailed. He began teaching Yale students Mende, and Cinque and his men began learning English.

Meanwhile, the case took a new twist when the Spanish government demanded that the *Amistad* and the cargo, including the Africans, be returned to Havana where the case could all be settled under Spanish law. Spain based these demands on the terms of treaties signed with the United States in 1795 and 1819.

Abolitionists immediately moved to block the return of the Africans to Cuba, arguing that they had been illegally taken out of Africa. In response, Cuban officials presented documents declaring that the fifty-three Africans were "ladinos," which meant they had arrived in Cuba before 1817 and the outlawing of slave transport. The papers were obviously forged. None of the Africans spoke Spanish, which they would have learned had they been living there that long, and the children, all under twelve, weren't even born in 1820.

The U.S. District Court trial opened in November 1839, but due to political pressure from President Martin Van Buren's administration, the case was de-

"Trial of the Amistad *Captives," by Hale Woodruff, c. 1940.*

layed until January 1840. Meanwhile, Spain kept the pressure on, and Van Buren simply wanted the issue to go away. On January 8, 1840, the *Amistad* Africans' trial opened in New Haven with Judge Judson presiding. By now the number of Africans had decreased to thirty-six. Several of them had died.

During the six days of testimony, Cinque won the respect of all those who saw and heard him give his dramatic account of being captured and taken from his homeland. Grabeau and Fuliwa also testified. These men gave Africans a face and a name. They had been farmers, artisans, and members of a society with principles and laws equal to any civilized nation.

"We are men, too," said Cinque. Judge Judson stunned the court when he agreed. Judson ruled in favor of the *Amistad* Africans. Gedney and Meade were granted salvage rights to the ship and cargo — but not the Africans, whom Judson declared "were born free and ever since have been . . . and still are free and not slaves." Judge Judson was commended for his actions, because he obviously resisted great pressure from the president to bring in a verdict against the Africans. Van Buren must have been surprised and embarrassed by the decision, because he had a ship waiting in the harbor at New London to transport the Africans to Havana.

Cinque understood enough English to know that they had won. But the struggle wasn't over yet. Spain wouldn't drop the case. Therefore the case was taken to the United States Supreme Court in Washington, D.C., February 20, 1841. Once again abolitionists were concerned about the makeup of the court. Five of the justices were from the South and slaveholders.

The abolitionists needed a person of national stature to join the defense team. Baldwin and others approached John Quincy Adams, the former president of the United States (1825–1829), who was also the son of President John Adams. Known to all as "Old Man Eloquent," Adams was against slavery, but unlike most abolitionists, he advocated gradual emancipation by means of constitutional amendments. At age seventy-three, Adams was reluctant to take on the case. After all, he argued, it had been thirty years since he had fought a case through the Supreme Court. The challenge was tempting. Few were surprised when he took the case.

What must the Southern justices have been thinking when they heard Baldwin argue that "The Africans' violent action to liberate themselves from their captors was not a crime, but the justifiable act of free men." Besides, he added, the Africans had never legally been slaves under Spanish law.

When his turn came to speak, John Quincy Adams attacked the Van Buren administration for its "shameful, unconstitutional interference in the *Amistad* case." He compared Cinque's act of "self-emancipation" to the actions of heroes who had overthrown tyrants in ancient Greece and Rome. With eloquence and a sure command of the law, Adams showed that the treaties cited by the federal government, including one he himself had negotiated while president, did not apply in this case.

The U.S. Supreme Court ruled in favor of the *Amistad* Africans on March 9, 1841. The Court found that the captives "by the law of Spain itself, are entitled to their freedom," because they had been "kidnapped and illegally carried to Cuba, and illegally detained and restrained on board the *Amistad.*" They were not property, but free individuals, therefore the Supreme Court ordered their immediate release.

Cinque and his friends could breath a long sigh of relief. Throughout Connecticut, church bells rang. Men, women, and children cheered. By their carriage and demeanor these proud young Africans had helped sway public opinion. People who normally weren't interested in the slavery debate had become interested in the *Amistad* Africans. They cared very much about what happened to them. Their pictures were drawn; they were studied and painted by artists. Cinque's portrait captured the spirit of the slave rebel, filled with dignity and a powerful will.

With thanks and gratitude, Cinque presented a Bible to John Quincy Adams in appreciation for his work. Kali, one of the Mende men who had learned to write in English, wrote, "We thank you very much because you make us free."

Released from custody after two years, the Afri-

John Quincy Adams, who argued the Amistad *case before the Supreme Court.*

cans were invited to live in Farmington in quarters that had been built especially to house them. The women and girls lived in private homes. Meanwhile, Cinque began speaking at abolitionist meetings, telling the story of the *Amistad* capture. Crowds paid a good price to see him and to hear him talk. Although Cinque could speak English, he hardly ever spoke it publicly. He told his story in Mende and used an interpreter. Some considered these lectures demeaning, but Cinque was raising money for their return home. There was no shame in that.

At last they had raised enough money. After an emotional farewell service at the Farmington Congregational Church, in which many townsfolk took part, in November of 1841 the Africans at long last set sail from New York for their homeland. It was especially moving that Cinque said his farewells in English.

Little is known about what happened to the *Amistad* Africans after they arrived home in January 1842. Margru, one of the girls, returned to America to study at Oberlin College in Ohio. She then went back to Africa to teach at the mission in Sierra Leone. Several of the men visited the American missionaries periodically. From them word was received that Cinque had found his way home and was living happily with his wife and family. The long night of his captivity was finally over.

9

HARRIET TUBMAN AND THE UNDERGROUND REBELLION

A favorite story among plantation slaves was about a runaway who was being chased by his master when suddenly the slave disappeared. It was as if the fugitive had found an *underground road.* This story is perhaps the origin of the term Underground Railroad, which was neither underground nor a railroad. Instead, it was the name of an elaborate system of secret escape routes runaways used to reach freedom. Those who helped escapees were called "conductors," and the safe houses where slaves were given help along the way were called "stations." Fugitives were hidden in attics, basements, in secret passageways, and tunnels. They traveled using forged free papers, phony passes, and disguises. Men disguised themselves as women and women disguised themselves as men. Conductors used all kinds of daring schemes to help runaways reach freedom.

Quakers played a prominent role in the runaway system, and so did other groups, such as the Wesleyan Methodists, Unitarians, Jews, and Roman Catholics. However, historians have overlooked the role African Americans played in this movement. According to John Hope Franklin, a noted African-American historian and teacher, prior to 1830 the Underground Railroad was not an organized part of the abolitionist movement. Yet slaves had been running away for two centuries. And "once free, these fugitives reached back to help others escape to freedom." So it is more accurate to say that "it was black courage and perseverance, and the spirited and enthusiastic support of whites, that brought many men, women, and children out of slavery."

Those who risked their lives and personal safety to become part of this active group of rebels are among America's most honored heroes. In the history of the Underground Railroad no one is more representative of this kind of rebel than Harriet Tubman who, for over ten years, was one of the most successful conductors on the Underground Railroad.

Biographies have made Harriet seem larger than life, and in some ways she was. But physically, Harriet was a short woman who stood a little over five feet.

She was born in 1820 or 1821. Harriet Green and Ben Ross were her parents, but they all belonged to Mas' Brodas who owned a plantation in Bucktown, Maryland. They named her Araminta or "Minty" for short, and she grew up with eleven brothers and sisters listening to songs and stories told in the quarters.

When she was six years old, Minty was hired out by her master to work for a woman she called "Miss

Susan." Minty's job was to keep the baby quiet, but when she couldn't do it — which was often — Miss Susan beat her with a whip.

Curious about the taste of sugar, Harriet took a lump from the sugar bowl. Miss Susan caught Minty and accused the girl of stealing. Minty hid behind the pigpen to escape the terrible beating she knew was in store for her. Several days later, when she finally returned, Miss Susan took her back to the Brodas plantation complaining that she wasn't worth the six pennies she paid for Minty. Little Minty had survived her first rebellious act. It was the beginning of her long career as a rebel against slavery.

Normally, unruly slaves were sold. But Minty was so small, she was assigned to the fields, where she learned to chop and hoe cotton alongside her brothers. But before long she was hired out again to the James Cooks.

Mrs. Cook was a weaver, and Mr. Cook was a trapper. When Minty couldn't make her fingers learn how to weave, Mr. Cook took Minty out into the woods with him to check the traps. What a surprise to learn that there were no ghosts in the woods! The overseers always told black children that story to keep them from running away. Now she knew better.

Minty overcame her fear of darkness and learned the sounds and smells of the woodlands and fields and how to move quietly through the brush. She also

Harriet Tubman, conductor on the Underground Railroad.

learned to identify the stars — especially the North Star — and to find moss on the north side of a tree. All this she put in her head. She didn't know it then, but this information would save her life one day.

The work was hard, but she didn't mind, because she was learning so much. But, working in the cold and being wet most of the time made her sick. When she told Cook she didn't feel well, he accused her of being lazy and insisted that she work that day. By evening Minty was burning with fever. Cook rushed her back to the plantation because he didn't want her to die. Brodas could demand payment for the loss of his "property."

Minty probably had pneumonia but her mother knew how to treat sicknesses. With loving hands, her mother prepared a salve and rubbed it on Minty's chest. Soon the fever broke, and Minty got better and grew strong.

One day when she was sixteen, Minty interfered with the overseer who was chasing a runaway. He hurled a heavy iron weight that knocked the girl unconscious. For eight months Minty lingered between life and death in a coma. Mama Harriet did all she could to heal the wound that had gashed open her child's head. Once again Minty recovered, but she was never the same. She even changed her name to Harriet in honor of her mother.

After the blow to her head, Harriet would sometimes stop in the middle of a sentence and stand for a few minutes stone-still as if asleep. Then coming around she would pick up her conversation right where she left off. Her symptoms suggest that she may have had a mild form of epilespy brought on by the blow to her head. But back then, people thought Harriet was just prone to spells or fits.

Since early childhood, Harriet had believed in dreams and omens, but as she grew older she shared them more with her mother. In one dream she saw a line dividing slavery from freedom. On one side she saw people holding out their hands to her and calling her "Moses." Harriet believed God had a plan for her. Mama Harriet believed it, too. "God will send me a sign," Harriet said.

In time, Harriet married John Tubman, a free man. She continued to work in the fields. Harriet was physically very strong, as strong as a man. Sometimes her master had Harriet demonstrate her strength by pulling the load of an oxen or mule. It was degrading and humiliating, but Harriet had no choice. She had to obey her master.

One day Harriet discovered that she was going to be sold into the "Deep South." That night, she prayed, and by morning she knew the answer. She would run away. When she told John Tubman, he tried to discourage her. Harriet turned to her brothers. They set out but they were so frightened they decided to return to the plantation. Harriet returned, too.

The next time, she decided, she would go alone. During the summer of 1849, Harriet ran. She didn't say good-bye to anyone — not even John. She stood outside her parents' shack and sang a song, hoping they would hear it and remember that it was her way of saying good-bye.

When that old chariot come,
I'm going to leave you.
I'm bound for the Promised Land,
Friends, I'm going to leave you.

Harriet made it to the home of a Quaker woman several miles away, who had befriended her when Harriet was a young girl. After resting and eating, Harriet was slipped away to the next safe house. With the help of others, Harriet inched along on this invisible highway to freedom. Within weeks Harriet was in Philadelphia, where she was free . . . really free.

After a while, Harriet made contact with a black man named William Still who was secretary of the Philadelphia Vigilance Committee. This is where runaways not only sought safety but where they came to see if they could find out news about their families and to meet other runaways and hear about their bold escapes.

Harriet no doubt heard about Henry "Box" Brown, who was shipped from Richmond to Philadelphia by the Adams Express Company in a box. The story of the Crafts must have been exciting to hear about. William and Ellen Craft escaped in one of the most ingenious plans ever devised by fugitives. Ellen, who was a fair-skinned black, posed as the master of William. To keep from having to speak, Ellen pretended to be too ill and frail to socialize. William explained that his master was on his way North to receive treatment. Though they narrowly escaped detection, the sham worked and the Crafts made it to freedom and became vocal abolitionists.

Harriet was most impressed with the conductors

Henry "Box" Brown was shipped to freedom in a crate.

on the Underground Railroad. She never tired of hearing stories about their exploits. Levi Coffin, a Quaker from Indiana, helped three thousand slaves escape. Calvin Fairbanks, who had learned to hate slavery while a student at Oberlin, went throughout the South, beginning in 1837, helping slaves to escape. Working with a white woman from Vermont known only as "Miss Webster," slaves posed as her servants and she escorted them to freedom. Fairbanks boasted that none of his escapees were ever caught, but he was captured and served seventeen years in prison for his work.

Conductors were found not only in the North. John Fairfield, son of a Virginia slaveholding family, learned to despise the system. He helped several slaves to escape from his own father's plantation, before moving to a free state. Fairfield posed as a slaveholder and went throughout Louisiana, Alabama, Mississsipi, Tennessee, and Kentucky arranging for mass escapes. Sometimes he took them all to Levi Coffin who arranged for them to be helped the rest of the way. Fairfield's greatest triumph was helping twenty-eight slaves to freedom by organizing them into a funeral procession.

It is possible Harriet might have met Jane Lewis of New Lebanon, Ohio, who was responsible for rowing fugitives across the Ohio River and Elijah Anderson, who from 1850 to 1857, led hundreds of people to freedom before dying in prison for his ac-

Josiah Henson escaped to freedom, and then returned to help others.

tions. She admired John Mason and Reverend William Mitchell who were also conductors who ushered hundreds to freedom. David Ruggles in New York had been the conductor who greeted Frederick Douglass and helped him on his way to New Haven, Connecticut. But it was Josiah Henson who inspired Harriet the most, because after escaping to freedom, he risked everything by returning to the South to personally help others.

Harriet worked for two years in Philadelphia and saved her money. She visited with Still and his group regularly, gaining courage from their work. Then word came that the movement was in serious trouble. A tougher Fugitive Slave Law had been passed. Runaways could be hunted into free territory and taken back to slavery. The only safe place for them was Canada or Mexico.

That meant the Underground Railroad had to be extended further north into Canada. Stations opened in Battle Creek, Michigan; Buffalo, New York; Beloit, Wisconsin; and other points north. Another route was set up moving through Texas and across the border into Mexico. Some slaves ran away as far as what is now Washington State and lived among Native Americans.

The Fugitive Slave Act turned more people into abolitionists than it stopped. Northerners resented bounty hunters coming into their communities insisting that they be helped in their slave catching. Most people wanted no part of it.

Harriet's freedom was in jeopardy, too. She could go to Canada or Mexico, but she wanted to become more involved. She wasn't a speaker like Frederick Douglass, James W. C. Pennington, Sojourner Truth, or Henry Highland Garnet; she wasn't a writer like David Walker, William G. Allen, William Lloyd Garrison; and she wasn't an organizer such as Sarah Parker Remond or David Ruggles. What could she do? She decided to follow Josiah Henson's example and became a conductor on the Underground Railroad.

"I can't die but once," she replied when people tried to tell her about the dangers of her mission.

Harriet's first trip back to Maryland's eastern shore was in 1850.

When that old chariot come,
I'm going to leave you.
I'm bound for the Promised Land,
Friends, I'm going to leave you.

She went back to get her sister first, and then her brother, and two other slaves. The first person she wanted to see was John Tubman, her husband. He now loved someone else and had moved her into his

Harriet Tubman (far left) and some of the slaves she led to freedom.

house. Brokenhearted, Harriet started to make a fuss. Then she realized her personal anger and hurt should not ruin it for everybody. She tucked away her hurt and sorrow and focused on what she had to do. Harriet never asked others to do what she herself could or would not do.

Nineteen times she went back to the South.

When that old chariot come,
I'm going to leave you.
I'm bound for the Promised Land,
Friends, I'm going to leave you.

She brought out men, women, and children, young and old, anybody with a burning desire to be free. She took them out of bondage and on up into Canada. Those who went with Harriet had to understand that she was not going to risk the life of the whole group because one person wanted to turn around. "I shoot the person who gives out," she told them before they started.

Many years later, an interviewer asked Harriet if she really would have done that. "Yes," she replied without hesitation, "if he (or she) was weak enough to give out, he'd be weak enough to betray us all, and all who had helped us; and do you think I'd let so many die just for one coward man."

"Did you ever have to shoot anyone?"

She smiled, then began her answer. "A man gave

out the second night we were out; his feet were sore and swollen, he couldn't go any further; he'd rather go back and die." Nothing could convince him to continue. That's when Harriet said, "Shoot him." When he heard her give the order, the reluctant runaway "jumped right up and went on as well as any body, made it right on to freedom." No, Harriet never lost a person.

Times were often miserable and tiring. Sometimes people had babies and she had to keep them quiet by giving them laudanum, a sedative. Once when she was on a trip to the South, Harriet ran into one of her old masters. She was so bold she spoke to him, but he didn't recognize her in disguise.

Except for one sister, she led out all her family, including her old parents and hundreds of strangers. Her efforts didn't stop once they reached Canada, either. She collected clothing, organized runaways into societies, and she was always occupied with plans for their benefit. African Americans called her the Moses of her people. Slaveholders called her a nuisance and put a hefty bounty on her head — $40,000 dead or alive! They never caught her.

During the Civil War, Harriet served as a spy and a nurse for the Union Army. After the war, she moved to Auburn, New York. Later she turned her home over to the African Methodist Episcopal Zion Church to be used as a home for the needy. Harriet died in 1913 at the age of ninety-three.

10

JOHN BROWN'S RAID AT HARPERS FERRY

It was 1859. The nation was divided over slavery and there seemed to be no compromise that either side could live with. Historically, when a nation has been pulled taut by internal struggle, it can take only one small incident to set off a chain of responses that can eventually lead to civil war.

A racially mixed group of twenty-one men attacked the armory at Harpers Ferry. They were quickly captured, tried, and executed for murder and treason. It seemed hardly worthy of a footnote in history, except that the raid was led by a radical abolitionist, in Virginia, in 1859. This event was that one small incident that set off a chain of responses that eventually led to the war between the states.

The rebel leader was John Brown, who was born May 9, 1800, the same year Nat Turner was born. Brown's parents, Owen and Ruth Mills Brown, were simple, hard-working people, devoutly religious and vehemently opposed to slavery. In 1805, the Browns moved to Hudson, Ohio, about twenty-five miles from Cleveland. Ruth Brown died when John was eight and the boy never stopped grieving for her.

When his father remarried, young John wasn't able to accept his stepmother right away.

Brown's first contact with slavery came when he was not yet sixteen. While on a cattle drive, he visited the home of a slaveholder in Indiana. Brown believed the man to be decent until he saw the man handle his slave. Brown noticed that the slave had been beaten so often and so hard he cowered when a hand was raised to him even in kindness. No human being should have to live under such tyranny, Brown decided. Upon leaving that place, Brown made the decision to devote his life to ending slavery.

To prepare himself for the struggle, Brown decided to study for the ministry. He went to school for a while in New England where abolitionism was strongest. An eye infection and the lack of money forced him to return to Ohio before his studies were concluded. Within the year Brown married Dianthe Lusk, "a remarkably plain" woman who died in 1832 after giving birth to their seventh child. Brown soon married Mary Ann Day, and together they had thirteen more children. To keep his large family fed, Brown worked at tanning, surveying, and farming. But he was generally unsuccessful.

Several of his older sons went out West where there were more opportunities. Meanwhile, in 1854, the Kansas-Nebraska Act had opened the western territories to slavery. Pro-slavery "Border Ruffians" clashed brutally with anti-slavery "Jayhawkers" over

John Brown led the raid on Harpers Ferry.

the extension of slavery into Kansas and Nebraska. The two opposing sides frequently clashed and for the next few years Kansas was the scene of one atrocity followed by another. Kansas became known as "Bleeding Kansas."

Brown's sons joined the Free-Soil cause, and in May 1855 their father joined them. This was John Brown's first opportunity to strike a blow against slavery and he did so with a fury. Pro-slavery forces sacked and burned parts of the town of Lawrence, Kansas, in May 1856. Brown's group retaliated and brutally killed five pro-slavery sympathizers at Pottawatomie Creek. Branded a murderer, he was thereafter known as "Bloody Brown" by some and "Pottawatomie Brown" by others. It was a time of extremes.

Returning to Ohio, Brown immediately began putting into action a plan he had designed before leaving for Kansas. He wanted to capture the arsenal at Harpers Ferry, Virginia (now West Virginia), then retreat into the mountains and establish a maroon community of runaways. From this maroon stronghold, they could raid plantations and lead slaves to freedom. Located high in the forested mountains, it would be easy to defend, just as the maroons had done in Jamaica.

Brown needed money to begin his mission, and he also needed recruiters. John E. Cook, Aaron D. Stevens, and John H. Kagi, men from his Kansas forces, were the first to join him. Cook went to Harpers Ferry as a spy in the fall of 1858. And Stevens and Kagi began carefully selecting other men.

Word spread among abolitionists that someone was planning a grand attack on slavery. The particulars were fuzzy, but specific enough to spark interest among the young and impatient.

Charles H. Langston might have been one of those who joined Brown, but he had already gotten himself involved with a group of anti-slavery men near Oberlin, Ohio. John Price, a black fugitive, had been captured by slave catchers and was about to be placed on a train to be taken back to Kentucky, but Langston's group snatched him from his captors and spirited him off to Canada. Since the men were in violation of the Fugitive Slave Law, thirty-seven of them were identified and indicted. Charles Langston, one of the only two men brought to trial, was tried and convicted in 1859. Langston spoke to the crowded courtroom saying: "If, for doing what I did . . . I am to go to jail six months and pay a fine of a thousand dollars, according to the Fugitive Slave Law . . . I . . . say that I will do all I can for any man thus seized and held, though the inevitable penalty hangs over me!" The judge gave him twenty days in jail and fined him a hundred dollars.

Among the cheering spectators in the crowd that day were Lewis Sheridan Leary and John A Copeland, Jr., who had also taken part in the rescue. Leary was a saddler and harness maker, who had come to Oberlin as a fugitive from South Carolina. Copeland, who was Leary's nephew, was a free man who had come to Ohio to study at Oberlin. They were both in their twenties. Both had made up their minds to join Brown at Harpers Ferry.

Brown was not having very much success with recruiting. He had held a meeting in Canada to lay out his plans for the abolition of slavery, and there were a few who made commitments. Brown felt if he could get leading black abolitionists to lend their voice to his cause, others might be drawn in. He approached Harriet Tubman who expressed a desire to help, but later declined due to illness. Frederick Douglass tried to convince his good friend that his plan could never work. There were far more people willing to give Brown money and moral support than were willing to enlist in his army.

But the old warrior was undaunted. Brown went to Harpers Ferry, arriving July 3, 1859. With him were two of his sons, and another Kansas veteran, Jeremiah Anderson, the grandson of a slaveholder. John Cook, who had been there for almost a year, knew the lay of the land. He had learned that there were 150 free blacks working in Harpers Ferry and about 150 slaves. In the surrounding counties there were approximately 18,000 slaves. It was from these men that Brown hoped to swell his numbers. Cook had rented the Kennedy farm which would serve as a hideout for the raiders. It was located on the Maryland side of the river, some five miles north of the town.

By 1859 Harpers Ferry was the site of the United States Armory and Arsenal. George Washington, as a young surveyor, had visited Harpers Ferry, and considered it the "most eligible spot on the [Potomac] river" for an armory. "There was plenty of water for power, and iron ore; hardwood trees would insure a steady supply of hardwood for charcoal to fuel the forges, and it was inland to be secure from foreign invasion." Part one of Brown's plan was to seize that arsenal.

For several months Brown and his men moved among the 3,000 residents of Harpers Ferry, attending one or several of the churches there or eating at Wager House. One by one the men began to arrive at the Kennedy farm. Watson Brown and William and Dauphin Thompson came in on August 6, followed the next week by Aaron Stevens and Charles Plummer Tidd. Canadian-born Stewart Taylor and two Iowa brothers, Edwin and Barclay Coppoc, who were Quakers, found their way to the farm by early September. Twenty-year-old William Leeman came down from Maine.

Out of Virginia's Shenandoah Valley came Dangerfield Newby, a free black man, whose wife, Harriet, and seven children were slaves. He had worked and saved money to buy their freedom. When he approached his wife's master, the master changed the asking price. Then a distressing letter came from Harriet, saying she was about to be sold to a planter in Louisiana and the children scattered. Newby was a desperate man whose hatred for slavery was as passionate as his love for his family. Inside his pocket was Harriet's last letter, pleading with him: "Buy me and the baby, that has just commenced to crawl, as soon as possible, for if you do not get me somebody else will. . . . Oh dear Dangerfield, come this fall without fail . . . I want to see you so much that is the one bright hope I have before me."

Osborne Anderson, a thirty-three-year-old free black, had met Brown at the Canada meeting and

Dangerfield Newby was the first to die at Harpers Ferry.

had promised to support his cause. True to his word, Anderson showed up in late August.

Because so many people knew about Brown's plan, it was bound to be betrayed. In August, Secretary of War John B. Floyd had received an unsigned letter stating "the existence of a secret association having for its object the liberation of the slaves at the South by a general insurrection." Brown was named as its leader and an armory in Maryland was named as the proposed target. First, Floyd didn't think anybody could dream up such an impossible scheme, and the informant was mistaken about the arsenal being in Maryland instead of Virginia. Floyd put the letter away, only to remember it later.

Brown was disappointed in the number of men who had answered the call. Hoping to garner some support, Brown met secretly with Frederick Douglass at Chambersburg, Pennsylvania. Once more Douglass tried to convince Brown not to go through with his plan.

When Douglass was sure there was nothing he could do to stop the old rebel, he shook his hand and parted. At the meeting was a fugitive slave from South Carolina named Shields Green. When Douglass and Brown agreed to disagree, Douglass asked Green what he planned to do. Green answered simply, "I b'lieve I'll go wid de ole man."

Leary and Copeland and Francis Merriam arrived at the farm two days before the raid was to take place.

Shields Green, one of the six survivors captured after John Brown's raid.

The air was crisp and still. Fall was marching down the mountain, changing the color of the leaves as it progressed day by day. Brown's army numbered twenty-one. Nineteen of them were under thirty; three were not yet twenty-one. Sixteen were white and five were black.

Brown announced the date for the attack: October 16, 1859. The night before, they ate, told stories about past victories, then Brown spoke to them in a quiet, deliberate way. He cautioned them:

> *You all know how dear life is to you . . . consider what the lives of others are to you; do not, therefore, take the life of anyone if you can*

possibly avoid it, but if it is necessary to take life in order to save your own, then make short work of it.

Some of his men, according to Osborn Anderson, visited blacks in the quarters and revealed the plan to them. "One old mother," he said later, "white-haired from age and borne down with the labors of many years in bonds, when told of the work in hand, replied: 'God bless you! God bless you!' She then kissed the party at her house, and requested all to kneel, which we did, and she offered prayer to God for his blessing on the enterprise, and our success."

The next day, Sunday, October 16, Brown put his

Osborn Anderson escaped and lived to give an account of the raid.

plan into action. For the most part it was a disaster. Brown was successful in capturing the arsenal and took several hostages. But he allowed himself to be trapped. His attempts at negotiation were not from a point of strength but weakness. There was no way for him to get out of the building into which he and his men had been maneuvered. By Monday morning, the men in the armory were trapped inside a fortress and totally vulnerable to the militia, volunteers, and federal forces — mobilized at amazing speed to put down what might have been a full-scale insurrection.

On Tuesday morning, October 18, the United States Marines led by then Colonel Robert E. Lee charged and broke the stronghold. The attempted insurrection had lasted no more than thirty-six hours.

John Brown was captured with five survivors: Stevens, one of the Coppoc brothers, Green, Copeland, and Watson Brown. Osborn Anderson escaped, and lived to fight in the Civil War. He died in 1871. Dangerfield Newby had been the first to fall. Leary also died.

During the initial investigation Brown was asked who had sent him. "No man sent me here," he said. "I want you to understand gentlemen . . . that I respect the rights of the poorest and weakest of colored people, oppressed by the slave system, just as much as I do those of the most wealthy and powerful. . . ."

Then he issued a warning: "I wish to say furthermore, that you had better — all the people of the

John Brown's trial in Jamestown, Virginia.

South — prepare yourselves for a settlement of that question that must come up for settlement sooner than you are prepared for it. The sooner you are prepared the better. You may dispose of me very easily; I am nearly disposed of now; but this question is still to be settled — this (N)egro question I mean — the end of that is not yet."

Brown and the other men were taken to James Town, Virginia (now West Virginia), on October 27. Their trial lasted three and a half days. Brown was found guilty and sentenced to be hanged on Friday, December 2, 1859. There was a massive attempt by abolitionist groups to save Brown's life. People sent hundreds of telegrams and letters asking for a jail sentence rather than death. But the verdict and the sentence stood.

On the day of his hanging, Brown gave his prison guard his last written message, which was:

> *I, John Brown, am now quite certain that the crimes of this guilty land will never be purged away but with blood. I had as I now think vainly flattered myself that without very much bloodshed it might be done.*

"John Brown Going to His Hanging," the famous painting by Horace Pippin.

A few minutes after eleven A.M. on December 2, 1859, John Brown walked calmly down the steps of Charles Town jail; he climbed into a horse-drawn wagon, and sat down on top of his coffin. No civilians were allowed near the execution site because there was fear that a rescue attempt might be made — but none came. The field was ringed with 1500 soldiers. Among them were a Virginia Military Institute professor who became known as General "Stonewall" Jackson, and John Wilkes Booth, the man who would assassinate President Abraham Lincoln.

Brown's last words were "Be quick." Seconds later he was dead. The soldiers cheered. It was a time of extremes.

Coppoc, Stevens, Copeland, and Green were tried and found guilty and sentenced to be hanged as well. Shields Green died looking his executioners in the eyes, refusing to flinch or yield. Young James Copeland wrote to his family in Oberlin from his cell:

> *I am not terrified by the gallows, which I see staring at me in the face, and upon which I am soon to stand and suffer death for doing what George Washington was made a hero for doing. . . . I imagine that I hear you, and all of you, mother, father, sisters and brothers, say — "No, there is not a cause for which we with less sorrow, could see you die."*

Southern slaveholders dismissed Brown as a lunatic and used him as the model for all abolitionists. Northern abolitionists made Brown a saint. Actually Brown was neither saint nor lunatic, but a man driven by his passions — a rebel. Some people hated Brown and everything he stood for. Other people sang his praises.

EPILOGUE

Defenders of slavery were surprised and angered when, no matter how much they tried, they couldn't dismiss John Brown as a lunatic. In fact, Brown became more dangerous in death than he ever was in life. Among anti-slavery sympathizers he was a martyr, a symbol of their total commitment to the eradication of slavery in the United States.

As the debate over slavery intensifed, the slaveholders sought support among Westerners who sided with them on the issue of states' rights, and Northern businessmen who relied upon the cotton markets. Still the South couldn't stop the mounting opposition against the slave system. What started as a small movement had, by the time of John Brown's execution, mushroomed into a strong political opposition. The South was particularly concerned about the newly formed Republican party and its candidate for president, Abraham Lincoln.

The Republican party was founded in 1854, and during the 1856 elections it had managed to seat several outspoken anti-slavery congressmen, among them Senator Charles Sumner from Massachusetts and Representative Thaddeus Stevens, congressman from Pennsylvania. As the 1860 elections approached, South Carolina threatened to secede from the Union unless John C. Breckenridge was elected president.

Breckenridge was the slaveholders' candidate. He took the position that a slave master should be allowed to keep slaves anywhere and in whatever state he lived. Virginia and other Southern Democratic delegates felt that Senator Steven A. Douglas from Illinois, who represented the Western faction of the Democratic party, was a good candidate, especially among Northern Democrats. As an advocate of states' rights, Douglas believed the right to keep slaves should be decided by state law, voted on by the people. He was vehemently opposed to the federal government becoming involved.

Abraham Lincoln, a lawyer from Springfield, Illinois, believed logically that a divided nation could not stand. During the Lincoln-Douglas debates, Lincoln pressed the issue further by saying the nation could not be half slave and half free. It would have to be all of one or the other — preferably free.

Such words were inflammatory, and the South accused Lincoln and the Republican party of being "revolutionary" and "rebels." In response the South increased both the frequency and volume of its own rebellious language — secession and war.

Even so, Lincoln was elected the sixteenth president of the United States, November 1860, at the age of fifty-five. He came to Washington under the threat of assassination and took the reins of a country that was speeding out of control.

Just as promised, South Carolina seceded from the Union on December 20, 1860. Other states followed its lead. Within months, the Confederate States of America was formed and Jefferson Davis was elected its president. There was even talk among some businessmen that New York should secede so trade with the South could continue. Known as "copperheads," these Southern sympathizers had little or no support.

But there were more than a few Northerners who opposed slavery, though not at the cost of a divided nation. They called for a "cooling off period." They were particularly relieved when Lincoln didn't rush in and free the slaves as many predicted he would. Instead, he tried to use reason and compromise with the South. Henry Garnet, Frederick Douglass, Sojourner Truth, Harriet Tubman, and other battle-weary rebels were more determined than ever. They insisted that it was no time for true abolitionists to retreat from the cause. "Slavery must be destroyed root and branch," said Sojourner Truth, a well-known African-American abolitionist and feminist. That idea was the foundation upon which rebels against slavery had been fighting for centuries.

Then on April 12, 1861, Confederate soldiers fired on federal troops at Fort Sumter, South Carolina, and the Civil War, also known as "the War of the Rebellion," began. The Civil War was fought over slavery. Economics, states' rights, and honor were all secondary reasons that lost their significance if slavery, the common denominator, was removed from the equation. Just as rebels had fought to end slavery, slaveholders and their sympathizers were equally convinced that they should fight to keep their slaves.

At first, African Americans were not allowed to join the Confederate or Union armies. Neither government felt comfortable arming black men. Frederick Douglass argued:

> *Once let the black man get upon his person the brass letter "US," let him get an eagle on his button and a musket on his shoulder and bullets in his pockets and there is no power on earth which can deny that he had earned the right to citizenship in the United States.*

After a great deal of pressure and after considering every possible alternative, on January 1, 1863, at 11:00 P.M., President Lincoln reluctantly signed the Emancipation Proclamation, freeing slaves in rebel states and allowing blacks to serve in the military. It was a simple document stating in part:

> *. . . all persons held as slaves within any state or designated part of a State, the people whereof shall then be in rebellion against the United States shall be thenceforth and forever free. . . . And I further declare and make known that such persons, of suitable condition, will be received into the armed service of the United States . . .*

The executive order was ignored by Southerners, who told blacks that "Yankees" were coming to kill them and their children, and that whites were fighting to protect them. But countless slaves ran away, joined the Union Army, and returned to fight to end slavery.

The war raged on for two more years; thousands died, thousands more were wounded. Fathers fought against sons at sunrise and at sunset in the fields and forests of Alabama, Georgia, and Missouri. Brothers fought against brothers in the mountains and along the rivers of Tennessee, Virginia, and Pennsylvania. Over 180,000 African Americans joined the Union Army in order to strike a death blow to the system.

The war ended in 1865. The South lay in smoldering ruins. The great plantation houses, the fields, the cities, and a way of life had come to an end. The African-American population had increased from the twenty indentured servants who had come into Jamestown, Virginia, in 1619, to four million freedmen who remained enslaved by overwhelming ignorance and staggering poverty.

To make sure they could not be legally re-enslaved by state laws, Congressman Thaddeus Stevens and Senator Charles Sumner pushed for the passage and ratification of the Thirteenth, Fourteenth, and Fifteenth Amendments, abolishing slavery in the United States forever and guaranteeing black men full rights of citizenship. Could the rebels rest in peace at last?

Hardly. Freedom proved to be a bittersweet victory. Although African Americans accepted the challenges and the responsibilities of their hard-earned citizenship, they soon learned that racism and discrimination could be just as cruel as slavery had been. Without justice there can be no freedom, and without freedom there can be no peace, for wherever there is oppression, there is bound to be resistance to it.

IMPORTANT DATES

1522 The first large-scale revolt of African slaves is on the plantation of Christopher Columbus's son, Diego, on the island of Hispaniola.

1546–1556 Significant revolts occur in the Caribbean, Mexico, Central and South America.

1619 Twenty blacks are brought into Virginia as indentured servants.

1638 Slave uprising in colonial Boston.

1641 Massachusetts becomes the first colony to legalize chattel slavery. Georgia is the last colony to legalize slavery in 1750.

1663 A plot between white indentured servants and slaves is discovered in Gloucester County, Virginia. They are betrayed by an indentured servant.

1712 Slave revolt in New York City.

1723 Slaves are accused of setting fires in Boston.

1725 Cudjoe sets up a maroon society in the Jamaican mountains.

1734 A rebellious plot is uncovered in Burlington, Pennsylvania.

1738 Cudjoe signs treaty with British governor, agreeing to return runaways in exchange for his autonomy.

1739 The Stono Rebellion.

1741 A series of fires lead New York officials to believe slaves were involved.

1775 First abolitionist society in the United States is started in Philadelphia on April 14, 1775.

November 7, 1775, Lord Dunmore, deposed royal governor of Virginia, promises freedom to all blacks who fight for the crown. Some blacks desert the plantations and join the British. On January 16, 1776, the Continental Congress approves George Washington's request to enlist slaves. No freedom is promised.

1777 Vermont first state to legally abolish slavery.

1791 Haitian Revolution begins with revolt of slaves in northern province (Saint-Domingue).

1793 First Fugitive Slave Law enacted by Congress, making it a criminal offense to help a runaway slave.

1800 Gabriel Prosser's revolt in Virginia.

Nat Turner and John Brown are born.

Denmark Vessey wins a lottery and purchases his freedom.

1803 April 7 Toussaint Louverture is found dead in a French prison.

1810–1850 The South loses more than 100,000 slaves, valued at more than thirty million dollars, on the Underground Railroad.

1811 Slave rebellion near New Orleans led by Charles Deslondes, a free black.

1816 Ft. Negro is destroyed by American ship.

The black Seminole leader, Garcia, is captured and hanged.

African Methodist Episcopal (A.M.E.) Church is formed.

1818 Andrew Jackson captures Pensacola.

1819 U.S. pays Spain 5 million dollars for Florida.

1820 Passage of the Missouri Compromise establishes the Mason-Dixon line and allows Missouri to enter the Union as a slave state and Maine as a free state.

1821(20) Harriet Tubman is born in Bucktown, Maryland.

1822 Denmark Vesey's planned rebellion betrayed by informer.

1823 Seminoles and their black allies are forced to live on a reservation in the Everglades.

1826 Seventy-seven slaves mutiny on a Mississippi River steamer and escape into Indiana.

1828 Morris Brown succeeds Richard Allen as Bishop of the A.M.E. Church.

1829 David Walker publishes *Walker's Appeal,* encouraging slaves to revolt and free blacks to fight against racism and discrimination.

1830 A group of North Carolina planters write a letter to the governor complaining that their slaves are becoming "almost uncontrollable."

David Walker dies. It is believed he was poisoned.

1831 William Lloyd Garrison publishes first issue of *The Liberator,* the most famous abolitionist newspaper.

Nat Turner's rebellion in Virginia.

1832–1843 The Seminoles refuse to move from their land. A ten-year war begins, led by Osceola.

1834 Slavery abolished in the British Empire.

1837 Elijah Lovejoy is martyred in Alton, Illinois, by a proslavery mob, when he refuses to stop publishing his anti-slavery newspaper. He dies when the mob burns his press.

1839 Seminoles and their black allies are forced to leave their homes in Florida and migrate to lands in Oklahoma Territory.

Slave rebels, led by Cinque, capture the *Amistad,* a Spanish slave ship.

1841 United States Supreme Court frees Cinque and the other *Amistad* rebels; they return to Africa.

In November there is a slave revolt on the *Creole,* which was en route to New Orleans from Hampton, Virginia. Rebels overpower the ship and sail it to the Bahamas where they are greeted as heroes.

1843 The Seminole War ends, but the Seminoles are not defeated.

1845 Seventy-five slaves from three Maryland counties arm themselves and march toward Pennsylvania. Many are killed and thirty-one are recaptured.

1848 Henry Highland Garnet reissues David Walker's *Appeal* and adds his own *Address* to it.

1849 Harriet Tubman escapes from slavery.

1850 Fugitive Slave Act is passed by Congress as part of the Compromise of 1850. Runaway slaves are no longer free once they reach a free state. They have to flee to Canada or Mexico where slavery is illegal.

Harriet Tubman makes her first trip back to the South as a conductor on the Underground Railroad.

1850–1860 Thousands of runaway slaves are helped to freedom via the Underground Railroad.

1854 Kansas-Nebraska Act repeals Missouri Compromise of 1820, and the Northern Territory is opened to slavery.

Republican party is organized.

1856 Pro-slavery forces burn parts of Lawrence, Kansas. John Brown and anti-slavery forces kill five pro-slavery sympathizers at Pottawatomie Creek.

1857 The Dred Scott decision by the U.S. Supreme Court denies citizenship to all blacks — whether they are slaves or free. Therefore, free blacks can't vote, hold public office, serve on juries, or even apply for a patent.

1859 John Brown with sixteen white men and five black men attacks Harpers Ferry, Virginia (now West Virginia), with the hope of establishing a maroon community in the mountains. He is captured and hanged on December 2, 1859.

1860 Abraham Lincoln elected president of the United States in November; South Carolina secedes from the Union on December 18, 1860.

1861 The "war of Southern rebellion" begins at Ft. Sumter in Charleston, South Carolina, on April 12.

1863 President Lincoln signs Emancipation Proclamation, on January 1, freeing slaves in the rebel states.

1865 On January 31, Congress passes the Thirteenth Amendment to the United States Constitution, which on ratification abolishes slavery in America.

BIBLIOGRAPHY

African Americans. "Voices of Triumph — Creative Fire." New York: Time-Life, 1994.

Aptheker, Herbert. *Abolitionism, A Revolutionary Movement.* Boston: G.K. Hall & Co., 1989.

Aptheker, Herbert. *Documentary History of the Negro People in the United States.* Vols. 1–5. New York: Citadel Press Book/Carol Publishing Group, 1951–1993.

Barry, Joseph. *The Strange Story of Harpers Ferry.* 10th Printing. Shepherdstown, W.Va: The Shepherdstown Register, Inc., 1988.

Bennett, Lerone, Jr. *Before the Mayflower: A History of Black America.* Chicago: Johnson Publishing Company, Inc., 1987.

Berlin, Ira, Barbara J. Fields, Steven F. Miller, Joseph P. Reidy and Leslie S. Rowland. *Slaves No More. Three Essays on Emancipation and the Civil War.* New York: Press Syndicate of the University of Cambridge, 1992.

Berry, Mary Frances. *Black Resistance/White Law.* New York: The Penguin Group, 1994.

Blassingame, John W. *The Slave Community: Plantation Life in the Antebellum South.* Revised and Enlarged Edition. New York: Oxford University Press, 1979.

Blassingame, John W. *Slave Testimony [Two Centuries of Letters, Speeches, Interviews and Autobiographies].* Baton Rouge: Louisiana State University Press, 1977.

Blockson, Charles L. *The Underground Railroad.* New York: Berkley Press, 1994.

Boles, John B. *Black Southerners, 1619–1869.* Lexington: University Press of Kentucky, 1984.

Botkin, B. A., ed. *Lay My Burden Down, A Folk History of Slavery.* New York: Delta/Bantam Doubleday Dell Publishing Group, Inc., 1973.

Boxer, C.R. *The Dutch Seaborne Empire, 1600–1800.* New York: Penguin, 1985.

Buckmaster, Henrietta. *Let My People Go.* Columbia: University of South Carolina, 1992.

Cantor, George. *Historic Landmarks of Black America.* Detroit: Gale Research, Inc., 1991.

Curtain, Philip D. *The Atlantic Slave Trade. A Census.* Madison: The University of Wisconsin Press, 1969.

Davis, Charles T. and Henry Louis Gates, Jr., eds. *The Slave's Narrative.* New York: Oxford University Press, 1985.

Genovese, Eugene D. *From Rebellion to Revolution.* Baton Rouge: Louisiana State University Press, 1979.

Grant, Joanne. *Black Protest. History, Documents, and Analyses. 1619 to the Present.* Second Edition. New York: Random House/Ballantine Books, 1991.

Gutman, Herbert G. *The Black Family in Slavery and Freedom. 1750–1925.* New York: Vintage Books/Random House, 1976.

Harding, Vincent. *There is a River. The Black Struggle for Freedom in America.* San Diego: Harcourt Brace Jovanovich, 1981.

Harper, Michael S. and Anthony Walton, eds. *Every Shut Eye Ain't Asleep. An Anthology of Poetry by African Americans since 1945.* Boston: Little, Brown and Company, 1994.

Hornsby, Alton, Jr. *Chronology of African-American History. Significant Events and People from 1619 to the Present.* Detroit: Gale Research Inc., 1991.

Kaplan, Sidney and Emma Nogrady Kaplan. *The Black Pres-*

ence in the Era of the American Revolution. [Revised Edition]. Amherst: The University of Massachusetts Press, 1989.

Katz, William Loren. *Black Indians, A Hidden Heritage.* New York: Atheneum/Macmillan, 1986.

Katz, William Loren. *Breaking the Chains.* New York: Macmillan Publishing Company, 1990.

Lee, George L. *Interesting People. Black American History Makers.* New York: Ballantine Books/Random House, Inc., 1989.

Litwack, Leon and August Meier, eds. *Black Leaders of the Nineteenth Century.* Urbana: University of Illinois Press, 1988.

McCain, Diana R. "Free Men: The Amistad Revolt and the American Anti-Slavery Movement." [Brochure, *New Haven Colony Historical Society,* 09-22-1989 thru 01-19-1990 & *The Connecticut Historical Society,* 02-04-1990 thru 06-17-1990] Connecticut Humanities Council.

Mullin, Gerald W. *Flight and Rebellion. Slave Resistance in Eighteenth Century Virginia.* New York: Oxford University Press, 1972.

Paiewonsky, Isidor. *Eyewitness Accounts of Slavery in the Danish West Indies [Also Graphic Tales of Other Slave Happenings on Ships and Plantations].* New York: Fordham University Press, 1989.

Paiewonsky, Isidor. *The Burning of a Pirate Ship,* La Trompeuse, *in the Harbour of St. Thomas, July 31, 1683, and Other Tales.* New York: Fordham University Press, 1992.

Polcovar, Jane. *What Was It Like? Harriet Tubman.* Stamford: Longmeadow Press, 1988.

Reynolds, Edward. *Stand the Storm. A History of the Atlantic Slave Trade.* Chicago: Elephant Paperbacks, Ivan R. Dee, Publisher, 1993.

Schwartz, Stuart B. *Slaves, Peasants, and Rebels.* Urbana and Chicago: University of Illinois Press, 1992.

Sherry, Frank. *Raiders and Rebels. The Golden Age of Piracy*. New York: (Quill) William Morrow, 1986.

Smith, Jessie Carney, with Casper L. Jordan, Robert L. Johns, eds. *Black Firsts [2,000 Years of Extraordinary Achievement]* Detroit: Visible Ink Press, 1994.

Snowden, Frank M., Jr. *Before Color Prejudice*. Cambridge: Harvard University Press, 1983.

Stampp, Kenneth M. *The Peculiar Institution. Slavery in the Ante-Bellum South*. New York: Vintage Books/ Random House, 1956.

Starobin, Robert S., ed. *Blacks in Bondage. Letters of American Slaves*. New York: Markus Wiener Publishing, 1988.

Stedman, John Gabriel. Edited by Richard Price and Sally Price. *Stedman's Surinam*. Baltimore: The Johns Hopkins University Press, 1992.

Styron, William. *The Confessions of Nat Turner*. New York: Signet Books/The New American Library, Inc., 1967.

Tibbles, Anthony, ed. *Transatlantic Slavery. Against Human Dignity*. London, United Kingdom: HMSO, 1994.

INDEX

Page references in italics indicate illustrations or photographs.

Abolitionism, 83–98. *See also* Slave rebellions
- Back to Africa movement and, 85–87
- Cinque and the *Amistad,* 116–117, 124, 126, 128
- Civil War and, 160–165
- Fugitive Slave Law and, 140
- Garnet, Henry Highland, 93–98
- Harpers Ferry raid, 144–159
- militancy of, 87–88
- origins of, 7–8, 83–85
- Quakers and, 16, 83–84
- Toussaint Louverture and, 50, 54
- Underground Railroad, 130–143
- United States and, 60, 70
- violence against, 107
- Walker, David, 88–93

Adams, John, 126
Adams, John Quincy, 70, 126–127, *128*
Africa, slavery in, 26
African Americans
- abolitionism and, 84–85
- Civil War and, 163–164
- Methodist Episcopal Church, 74–75
- Underground Railroad, 130–143

African captives, *15, 63*
African Methodist Episcopal Church. *See also* Methodist Episcopal Church
- formation of, 75
- hostility toward, 75–76
- outlawing of, 81
- Tubman and, 143

Allen, Richard, 74–75, *75,* 81
Allen, William G., 140
American Anti-Slavery Society, *84*, 85, 96–97
American Colonization Society, 85–86
American Revolution, 5, 6–7
Amistad, 113, 114, 115, *121, 124.* *See also* Cinque, Joseph
Anderson, Elijah, 138
Anderson, Jeremiah, 149
Anderson, Osborne, 151–152, 154, *154,* 155
Anti-slavery movement. *See* Abolitionism; Slave rebellions
Aptheker, Herbert, 83
Asi-yaholo. *See* Black Drink Crier (Seminole leader)

Back to Africa movement, 85–87, 90
Baldwin, Roger Sherman, 117, 121, 123
Baptiste, Simon, 44
Bennett, Thomas, 80
Biassou (rebellion leader), 46, 48

Black Drink Crier (Seminole leader), 34
Black Seaman's Act, 82
Blanco, Don Pedro, 120
Bonaparte, Napoleon (emp. of France), 52, 54, 56
Booth, John Wilkes, 158
Boston, Massachusetts, slave rebellion in, 21–22
Bowler, Jack, 63, 66
Brazil, 2, 12, 27
Breckenridge, John C., 161
British Guyana, slave rebellions in, 12
Brown, Henry "Box," 136–137, *137*
Brown, John (rebellion leader), 3, 144–145, *146,* 147–159
  abolitionism and, 147, 160
  arrest of, 155–156
  birth of, 144
  childhood of, 144–145
  education of, 145
  execution of, 157–159
  Harpers Ferry raid and, 147–155
  trial of, *156*, 156–157
Brown, Morris, 74, 81
Brown, Owen, 144
Brown, Ruth Mills, 144
Brown, Watson, 150, 155
Burlington, Pennsylvania, slave rebellion in, 22

Calhoun, John C., 80, 85
Caribbean Islands
  maroon communities in, 26–27
  slave rebellions in, 12–13
  slavery in, 1–2, *2,* 11–12, *12*
Catawba Indians, 63
Cato (Stono Rebellion leader), 3, 22–24
Chapman, Maria, 85
Charleston, South Carolina, 14
  African Methodist Episcopal Church, 76
  slavery in, 72–73
  Vesey's rebellion, 76–82
Child, Lydia Maria, 85
Christophe, Henri, 55, *55,* 56
Cinque, Joseph (rebellion leader), 10, 114, *115, 124*
  abolitionist movement and, 128
  African life of, 118–119
  enslavement of, 119–120
  leadership of, 116, 117, 120
  Middle Passage experience of, 120–121
  release of, 127–128
  trial of, 121–124, *124,* 125–127
Civil War (U.S.), 7, 28, 143, 160–165
Clay, Henry, 86
Cobb, Jeremiah, 109
Coffin, Levi, 138
Columbus, Christopher, 1, 13
Columbus, Diego, 13
Communication, among slaves, 17–18
Connecticut, slavery in, 14, 115
Constitution (U.S.)
  slavery abolished, 165
  Thirteenth Amendment, 2
Cook, James, 132
Cook, John E., 147, 148, 149
Copeland, John A., Jr., 148–149, 152, 155, 158
Copperheads, 162
Coppoc, Barclay, 150, 155, 158
Coppoc, Edwin, 150, 155, 158
Cornish, Samuel, 89–90
Covey, James, 123
Craft, Ellen, 137
Craft, William, 137
Cuba, 56
  maroon communities in, 27
  slavery in, 2
  slave trade and, 114, 120, 124
Cudjoe (maroon leader), 25–26, 27
Cuffy, Paul, 86, *86*

Dade, Francis, 36
Davis, Jefferson, 162

Declaration of Independence, 6, 7
Democratic party, 161
Deslondes, Charles, 69–70
Dessalines, Jean-Jacques, 53, 56, 57
Douglas, Steven A., 161
Douglass, Frederick, 85, 139, 140, 149, 152, 162, 163
Dutch Guyana, 25

Education, prohibition of, 7
Egypt (ancient), 1, 71
Emancipation Proclamation, 163–164
England. *See* Great Britain

Fairbanks, Calvin, 138
Fairfield, John, 138
Ferrer, *121*
Fifteenth Amendment, 165
Florida
  maroon communities in, 28, 30–40
  Seminole Wars, 36–40
  United States purchases, 33
Floyd, John B., 108, 110–111, 152
Forten, James, 85
Fort Negro, 31, 32, *32,* 33
Fort Sumter, South Carolina, 162–163
Fourteenth Amendment, 165
France
  Great Britain and, 57
  Haiti and, 5–6
  Prosser's rebellion, 62
  Saint-Domingue, 41, 48, 52–59
  Spain and, 48–51
Francis, Nathaniel, 105
Francis, Sam, 105
Franklin, John Hope, 131
Free blacks, abolitionism and, 8
Free-Soil movement, 147
French Guyana, 25
French Revolution, 5, 6–7
Fugutive slave clause, Native American treaties, 9, 30
Fugitive Slave Law, 7, 139–140, 148

Gabriel's rebellion (1800), 7
Garcia (maroon leader), 31–33
Garnet, George, 93
Garnet, Henry Highland, 8, 93–94, 93–98, *94,* 95–98, 140, 162
Garrison, William Lloyd, 85, 107, 140
Gedney, Thomas, 114, 115, 122, 125
Genovese, Eugene D., 2, 13, 30, 107–108
George II (king of England), 2
Georgia
  maroon communities in, 28, 30, 31
  slavery in, 14, 16
Gibbs, Josiah Willard, 123
Gray, Thomas R., 102–103
Great Britain, 2
  France and, 57
  Jamaica and, 26
  Saint-Domingue, 51–52
  War of 1812, 31, 32
Green, Beriah, 96
Green, Harriet, 131
Green, Shields, 152, *153,* 155, 158

Haiti, 10. *See also* Hispaniola; Saint-Domingue; Santo Domingo
  formation of, 5
  Prosser's rebellion and, 61, 63, 68
  slave rebellions and, 69–70
  Vesey, Denmark and, 71
Harpers Ferry raid, 144–146, *146,* 147–159
Harth, Hingo, 79
Hédouville, Gabriel, 52
Henson, Josiah, 139, *139*
Hernandez, Joseph, 37
Hispaniola, slave rebellions in, 13. *See also* Haiti; Saint-Domingue; Santo Domingo

Indentured servitude, slavery and, 16

Indian Removal Act, 34, 36
Informants, encouragement of, 9–10
Interracial marriage, 14, 31

Jackson, Andrew, 31–32, 33, 34, 36
Jackson, Thomas Jonathan "Stonewall," 158
Jamaica, 25–26
Jamestown, Virginia, 13
Jefferson, Thomas, 70
Jemmy. *See* Cato
Jesup, Sidney Thomas, 36, 37
Jocelyn, Simeon S., 117
John Horse (Seminole leader), 38
Johnson, Octave, 28–29
Judson, Andrew, 117, 121, 122, 125

Kagi, John H., 147, 148
Kansas-Nebraska Act, 145, 147

Langston, Charles H., 148
Laveaux, 49, 50, 51
Lawrence, Kansas, 147
Leary, Lewis Sheridan, 148–149, 152, 155
Leavitt, Joshua, 117
Leclerc, Charles, 54, 56
Lee, Robert E., 155
Leeman, William, 150
Lewis, Jane, 138
Lincoln, Abraham, 158, 160, 161–162, 163–164

Maitland, Thomas, 52
Mali, slavery in, 26
Maroon communities, 24, 25–40
  Fort Negro, 31, 32, *32*, 33
  Harpers Ferry raid and, 147
  Jamaica, 25–26
  life in, 28–29
  Native Americans and, 29–30
  North America, 27–28
  origins of, 25
  Saint-Domingue, 42–43
Maryland, slavery in, 14
Mason, John, 139
Mason-Dixon line, 70
Massachusetts, slavery in, 14
Massachusetts General Colored Association, 88, 90
Meade, Richard, 114, 115, 122, 125
Mende people (Africa), 118, *118*, 119–120, 129
  slavery and, 73–74
  Vesey, Denmark and, 73
Merriam, Francis, 152
Methodist Episcopal Church. *See also* African Methodist Episcopal Church
Mexico, 7
  slave rebellions in, 13
  Underground Railroad and, 140
Middle Passage
  conditions during, 112–113
  slave rebellions during, 112–129
Missouri Compromise, 70
Mitchell, William, 139
Monroe, James, 62, 65, 68, *69*, 80
Montes, Pedro, 114, 120
Moore, Putnam, 100
Moore, Sally, 100
Moore, Thomas, 100
Moses, 1, 61–62, 71, 111
Mott, Lucretia, 85
Mulattoes, Saint-Domingue, 41–42, 51, 52–53
Music
  African, *63*
  as communication, 17–18, 61–62

Nash, Gary B., 29
Native Americans
  Indian Removal Act, 34, 36
  maroon communities and, 29–30
  Prosser's rebellion, 63
  runaway slaves and, 9
  Seminole Wars, 33–40
  slave rebellions and, 8

Negro Abraham (Seminole leader), 38, *39*
Netherlands, slave trade and, 112
New Amsterdam. *See* New York, New York
Newby, Dangerfield, 150, 151, *151,* 155
Newby, Harriet, 150, 151
New Jersey, slavery in, 14
New Orleans, Louisiana, slave rebellion and, 69–70
New York, New York, 14, 21, 22
New York Manumission Society, 94
North America
  maroon communities in, 27–28
  slave codes in, 14–16
  slave rebellions in, 14
  slavery in, 2, 13–14
North Carolina
  maroon communities in, 28
  repression in, 4–5
  slavery in, 14, 16

Oklahoma, Indian Removal Act, 36, 39
Oneida Theological Institute, 96
Osceola (Seminole leader), *35,* 36–38

Parker, James, 105
Passive resistance, slave rebellions and, 17–19
Pennington, James, W. C., 140
Pennsylvania, 14, 22
Pétion, Alexandre, 56, *57*
Philadelphia Vigilance Committee, 136
Phillips, Wendell, 85
Phipps, Benjamin, 109, *109*
Pleasants, John Hampden, 110
Politics
  Civil War (U.S.) and, 160–165
  Fugitive Slave Law, 7, 139–140
  Kansas-Nebraska Act, 145, 147
  Missouri Compromise, 70
  slave codes and, 14–16
  slavery and, 8–9, 14
Portugal, 27, 120
Poyas, Peter, 76, 77, 79, 80, 81
Price, John, 148
Prioleau, John C., 79
Pritchard, Jack, 76–77
Prosser, Gabriel (rebellion leader), 3, 7, 10, 61–70, 71
Prosser, Martin, 61
Prosser, Solomon, 61, 63, 66–67
Prosser, Thomas, 61
Purvis, Robert, 85

Quakers
  abolitionism and, 16, 83–84, 136, 150
  Underground Railroad and, 130, 138

Racism
  slavery and, 15–16, 18
  Walker, David, 90
Rape, slave rebellions and, 107–108
Rebellions, against slavery, 1. *See also* Slave rebellions
Reese, Giles, 100, 105
Remond, Sarah Parker, 140
Republican party, formation of, 160–161
Resistance. *See* Abolitionism; Passive resistance; Slave rebellions
Rhode Island, slavery in, 14
Rice cultivation, 31
Richmond, Virginia, Prosser's rebellion, 62, 64–68
Ridley, Thomas, 106
Rigaud, André, 51, 53
Rochambeau, 56
Ross, Ben, 131
Ruggles, David, 139, 140
Ruiz, José, 114, 120
Runaway slaves
  costs to planters of, 24
  Fugitive Slave Law and, 7
  maroon communities and, 26
  Native Americans and, 9

Underground Railroad, 130
Walker, David, 90
Russwurm, John B., *89,* 89–90

Saint-Domingue. *See also* Haiti; Hispaniola; Santo Domingo
founding of, 41
slave rebellions in, 5, 12, *42,* 43, 46, 48–49
slavery in, 41–43
war for independence, 50–59
San Salvador, 1
Santo Domingo. *See also* Haiti; Hispaniola; Saint-Domingue
Scott, Winfield, 36
Selden, Joseph, 68
Seminole Nation, 9, 30–31
maroon communities and, 30–31
Osceola (Seminole leader), *35*
Seminole Wars, 36–40
Sheppard, Mosby, 65
Sherman, Roger, 117
Sierra Leone, 86, 118, *118,* 119–120, 129
Simon, Suzanne, 45
Slave codes, North America, 14–16, 21
Slave rebellions. *See also* Abolitionism
abolitionism and, 83–98. *See also* Abolitionism
Caribbean Islands, 12–13
Deslondes, Charles, 69–70
early, 20–24
fear of, 3–4, 7
leader of, *27*
Middle Passage, Cinque and the *Amistad,* 112–129
newspaper report of, *67*
numbers of, 2–3
passive resistance and, 17–19
Prosser's rebellion, 3, 7, 10, 61–70
punishment for, 4
repression and, 4–5, 7
Saint-Domingue, *42,* 43, 46–49
shipboard, *20*
South Carolina, 2
suicide and, 19–20, *20*
Turner's rebellion, 99–111
Vesey's rebellion, 76–82
Slavery
abolition of, 165
Caribbean Islands, 1–2, *2*, 11–12, *12*
conditions under, 8, 17–18, 100, 145
educational prohibition, 7
North America, 2, 13–14
politics and, 8–9
racism and, 15–16
rebellions against, 1. *See also* Slave rebellions
Saint-Domingue, 41–43, 50
Slave ships, *20*
Slave trade
Cuba and, 114, 120, 124
Middle Passage, slave rebellions during, 112–129
Netherlands and, 112
Portugal and, 120
Spain and, 120
Song, as communication, 17–18, 61–62
Sonthonax, Léger, 50, 52
South America, 13, 26–27
South Carolina
African Methodist Episcopal Church, 76
secession of, 162
slave rebellions in, 2, 4
slavery in, 14, 16, 72–73
Vesey's rebellion, 76–82
Spain
Amistad case and, 123–125, 127
Cuba and, 27
Florida sold by, 33
France and, 48–51
Saint-Domingue, 52
Santo Domingo, 53
slave trade and, 120
Spartacus, 1, 45
Stevens, Aaron D., 147, 148, 150, 155, 158
Stevens, Thaddeus, 161, 165

Still, William, 136
Stono rebellion (South Carolina, 1739), 3, 4, 22–23, *23,* 24
Storrs, Gervas, 68
Suicide, slave rebellions and, 19–20, *20*
Sumner, Charles, 160–161, 165
Supreme Court (U.S.), 121, 126, 127

Taino Indians, 41
Taylor, Stewart, 150
Thirteenth Amendment, 2, 165
Thompson, Dauphin, 150
Thompson, Smith, 121, 122
Thompson, Wiley, 36
Thompson, William, 150
Tidd, Charles Plummer, 150
Toussaint Louverture, 5, *6,* 10, *47,* 60
  birth of, 43–44
  childhood of, 44
  death of, 56, *58*
  education of, 44–45
  imprisonment of, 55–56
  Prosser's rebellion and, 61, 68
  slave rebellions and, 46, 48–49, 68–69, 71
  war for independence, 50–52
Travis, Hark, 105
Travis, Joseph, 100
Truth, Sojourner, 85, 140, 162
Tubman, Harriet, 10, *133, 141,* 149, 162
  birth of, 131
  childhood of, 131–132, 134–136
  death of, 143
  escape from slavery of, 136
  Underground Railroad and, 137–143
Tubman, John, 135, 141
Turner, Benjamin, 99, 100
Turner, Bridget, 99, 102
Turner, Cherry, 100
Turner, Nancy, 99
Turner, Nat (rebellion leader), 3, 4, 99–111, *101,* 144
  arrest of, 102, 109, *109,* 110
  birth of, 99
  childhood of, 99–100, 102
  execution of, 110
  rebellion of, 7, 102–103, *104,* 105–109
Turner, Samuel, 100

Underground Railroad, 7, 130–143

Van Buren, Martin, 124, 125, 126
Venezuela, slave rebellions in, 13
Vesey, Denmark (rebellion leader), 3, 10, 70
  African Methodist Episcopal Church, 75
  arrest of, 80
  biography of, 71–73
  education of, 71
  execution of, 81
  home of, *72*
  Methodism and, 73–74
  rebellion of, 7, 76–80
Vesey, Joseph, 61
Virginia
  maroon communities in, 28, 29
  Prosser's rebellion, 62, 64–68
  repression in , 4–5
  slavery in, 13–14, *14*
  Turner's rebellion, 102–103, *104,* 105–108, *108,* 109

Walker, David, 8, 88–93, 96, 97–98, 140
Walker's Appeal, 91, 91–93, 97–98
War of 1812, 31, 32
War of the Knives (Saint-Domingue), 53
Washington, George, 150
Weapons, prohibition of, 8
Wild Cat (Seminole leader), 38
Williams, Nelson, 105
Woolfolk, Ben, 64
Wright, Theodore S., 94

Art/Photo credits:

Photo research by Photosearch, Inc., New York.

Front cover art: *Cinque*, by Nathaniel Jocelyn, The Granger Collection.

Page 35: The Bettmann Archive; **Page 55**: Birmingham Art Gallery, Birmingham, England; **Page 146**: Boston Athenaeum; **Page 20**: The British Library; **Page 78**: Chicago Historical Society; **Page 63**: Colonial Williamsburg; **Page 133**: The Granger Collection; **Page 108**: Historical Pictures Service/Stock Montage, Chicago; **Pages 23, 72**: J. Michael Krouskop/Tradd Street Stock; **Pages 15, 101, 109**: Library of Congress; **Page 84**: Madison County Historical Society, Oneida, NY; **Page 128**: Metropolitan Museum of Art, Gift of I.N. Phelps Stokes, 1937 acc. #37.14.34; **Page 75**: Moorland-Spingarn Research Center, Howard University; **Pages 113, 118, 121, 124**: The New Haven Colony Historical Society; **Page 32**: North Wind Picture Archive; **Pages 53, 151, 154**: NPS, Harpers Ferry/Rieger Comms, Gaitersburg, MD; **Page 157**: The Pennsylvania Academy of the Fine Arts; **Page 42**: Roger-Viollet; **Pages 27, 58, 89, 91, 94, 115, 137**: Schomberg Center for Research in Black Culture, New York Public Library; **Page 141**: Sophia Smith Collection, Smith College; **Page 86**: State Historical Society of Wisconsin; **Page 67**: Valentine Museum, Richmond; **Page 104**: Virginia Historical Society; **Page 69**: Virginia State Library; **Pages 139, 156**: Western Reserve Historical Society.